Purpose

Sue Fitzmaurice

What they're saying about *Purpose*

Sue Fitzmaurice has such a way with words that they sneakily enter your mind, cut straight to the core of your soul with razor sharp precision – forcing you out from your comfort zone and straight into a showdown with the one person in this world you NEED to confront and challenge – your Self.

One of my favorite quotes from *Purpose: If there is Truth with a capital 'T' in the beliefs you hold dear then let that Truth stand the test of your openness to change. You cannot have a passionate life without openness, just as you cannot have a purposeful life without passion.*

J.V. Manning, author of The Other Side, and others

www.randomthoughtsandlotsacoffee.com

Sue asks the fundamental question *what is my purpose?* and proceeds to bravely light the way. The book's humanistic approach cleverly explores self-imposed limitations by dissecting tired beliefs and replacing them with empowering calls to action.

Sue's voice is an unflinching beacon of hope addressing hard topics such as depression, loss, shame, and fear. Her eloquent writing and glimpses into personal experience offer the reader a smart and modern portrait for understanding the direct connection between spirituality and creating a life of meaning.

Cindy Lamothe, writer, artist
www.crlamothe.com

Sue's style of writing draws you in on a journey of self-discovery. This book is for anyone struggling with understanding the meaning of life or what their purpose is. Through her own experience she offers the readers a wealth of information from exploring the obstacles standing in the way of their purpose to practical tools for living a life of purpose.

Di Riseborough, Intuitive Life Strategist; 'F-Word' Specialist, author of the best-selling book *Forgiveness: How to let go when it still hurts* ,
www.diriseborough.com

Sue is driven to help folks find their purpose in life. Using personal anecdotes, a grand and loving application of the Virtues, and a straightforward discussion of obstacles along your journey, she encourages a deep dive into the world of why you are here. The result: you, closer to your purpose.

Nancy Rainwater, Ph.D.
www.creatingwithintent.com

This book is such an inspiring and informative read. Sue Fitzmaurice certainly knows what she is talking about.

Lynda Field, author of *Weekend Life Coach; Weekend Confidence Coach; Instant Life Coach; and many more*
www.lyndafield.com

Would you like to know more about what your life purpose is? Sue Fitzmaurice has created a wonderful road map for you to discover, explore and implement exactly what calls out to you – right now! Her writing is smart, snappy and straight-to-the point, and will guide you in discovering your true purpose, every step of the way. If you desire to create a life that is meaningful and valuable, don't hesitate to get *Purpose* – there is a wealth of wisdom in there, waiting just for you!

Heather McCloskey Beck, author of the best-selling book *Take the Leap*

www.heathermccloskeybeck.com

Written in Sue's inimitable style, with clarity, humour and humility, this book is must read for anyone endeavouring to seek a greater understanding of how to live life with a greater sense of gusto. No matter what your age, status or background this little book with a big heart gets to the root of how to live a more fulfilling and purposeful life no matter where you are in your journey. *Purpose* is practical, insightful, down to earth and a cracking good read!

Caroline Ravenall, author of *A guide for the spiritual worrier/warrior*

www.carolineravenall.com

Sue Fitzmaurice's *Purpose* is a deeply beautiful, deceptively simple and profoundly comforting affirmation that our purpose is both changing and unchanging – and understanding the difference makes *all the difference.*

Cindy Ratzlaff, co-author of *Queen of Your Own Life*

www.queenofyourownlife.com

Sue Fitzmaurice brings the same wit, humor and honesty to *Purpose* that is present in all her writing.

When she writes early on *I'm not perfect at this yet,* Ms. Fitzmaurice is alerting the reader that letting go of making value judgements is a journey. With this one remark, she levels the playing field, shows her humanity and allows the reader to connect with her. We further engage with Sue while she recounts personal stories about her family's inner strength, living outside the box, courage, and following one's passion.

Many writers presenting thoughts about worthiness and finding one's purpose sound lofty and grandiose, like they're preaching from a pedestal. Not so with Sue. She presents complicated issues in an intelligent, clear cut manner coupled with an open approach that makes the journey to connecting to one's higher self and finding life's purpose easily accessible.

Personally meaningful and great read. Well done!

Ivy Tobin, actress and author of *My Life as a Doormat*

thesocietyforrecoveringdoormats.com

Purpose is the kind of book you wish you had had when you were starting out in life. Fortunately, it's never too late to live your purpose. Sue Fitzmaurice provides us with an insightful as well as inspirational road map for the journey.

Eleanor Brownn, author of *Mile 9*

www.EleanorBrownn.com

In *Purpose,* Sue Fitzmaurice breaks down that vague word into practical, logical advice. If there's a part of your mind that doesn't believe you have a purpose, it will have a healthy argument here to believe you truly do. ***Purpose*** delves into the mind to discover where it may be blocked and how to nudge it forward. Excellent advice and well worth the read.

Doe Zantamata, author of *Happiness in Your Life – Book One: Karma,* and others

www.happinessinyourlife.com

For Ruby & Madison, as always

Also by Sue Fitzmaurice

Fiction

Angels in the Architecture

Note to the Reader

In the main I employ *English* English. Those unused to this great language may stumble over the 'u' of neighbour and the verb of 'practise'. There is no word 'gotten' in the Queen's English and we politely 'minimise' without a 'z' (which we pronounce 'zed', by the way). Quotations from others are in the version of English of their nationality or first publication. Any other errors are indeed mine and I pray your forgiveness.

Contents

Introduction

At some point in your life, I hope you'll ask the question either *what is my purpose?* or *what is the purpose of life?* They are the most important questions you can ask, since it indicates you have some sense that life has meaning other than that we are born, we work from nine-to-five, we acquire things, we have a little fun, and then we die.

If you should first of all ask me the question *does life* have *a purpose?* then my answer will be a resounding *YES!* It becomes entirely academic then whether there is a difference between *believing* there is a purpose and *wanting* to believe there is a purpose. **The reality is we are more satisfied when we are living a purposeful life than when we are not.** We are happier, healthier and our relationships are better; period. It's irrelevant if some people like to say that life has no purpose – it's meaningless to think this, since a purposeful life is a better, happier life to live. You can argue about that unscientific conclusion, but the evidence of a purposeful life has most certainly been concluded scientifically, so I for one am happily making the leap to believing that life has a purpose.

The purpose of life is to live a life of purpose.

So what *is* the purpose of life? It's quite simple: it is to live a life of purpose. What is *your* purpose? It is taking what you love and what you're passionate about and making a difference; to make the world a better place by doing something you love. You may not even be very good at the thing that you're passionate about, although almost certainly you will become good at it if you love it enough.

Finding purpose though, and then living it, still seems to elude most of us. Even when we think we have it clear in our heads, it will escape sometimes and even trick us into thinking that's not it, that something else is 'it'.

So there's finding your purpose, and then there's holding onto it. And then there are the times when your purpose *does* change.

In school we're given the resources we need to pass exams to gain our high school qualifications. We are encouraged to think about what we're interested in and what we'd like to *be* when we leave school. If we don't think we're cut out for university or we're not interested in university, then most likely we're encouraged to *get a job*. If we do have some sense of a career – one that might involve tertiary study – **we are rarely if ever shown or told about this in terms of *purpose*.** *Job* or *career* are the overarching terms in use. And that's not surprising since *purpose* has definite connotations that are not generally a part of the lexicon of modern education or job and career-seeking.

Purpose goes beyond just what you're interested in. I'm interested in photography, but I don't want a career in it since it has no sense of purpose attached to it for me. I enjoy it, I appreciate it, I could even be quite good at it, but it's not my purpose. It *will* be someone's purpose – lots of people probably – but it's not mine.

Holding many of us in check is that on the way to achieving our purpose we all still have to pay bills, put food on the table, meet our obligations to our children, our communities and so on. This frequently – in fact almost always at some point – necessitates us having to do work that is *not* our purpose, but that supports us while we're going about working towards other goals. So it's worthwhile taking the view that **if it is getting us to where we want to be, it also forms a part of our purpose**, and there is little point in resenting it or hating it, even if we believe it is menial work that is somehow beneath us.

Your purpose will unfold with the positivity you put into your daily world.

Actually there is no work that is beneath anyone; at least that is one important perspective to consider. As long as you take a negative attitude towards the work you do, you will find it takes you longer to escape the work you don't enjoy so much. Your purpose will unfold with the positivity you put into your daily world. If you practice happiness, you will work more quickly towards your larger goals. If you understand that the work you do now is helping you along the path towards your greater goals, then you will appreciate it, you will be better at it, you will be happier with it, and you will move more speedily in the direction of your dreams.

Unless we're fortunate enough to have some very unique kind of education or upbringing that teaches us we need to find our purpose, then we will usually come to this concept of purpose from one or both of two particular directions: either we have just always *known* somewhere inside us that we have a purpose; or we experience increasing frustration from the work we are doing, or from the nature of life about us and the stage of life we're at, and eventually hit on the idea that we lack purpose and we'd like to have some.

Whichever direction we come at it, we usually experience the need for purpose as a spiritual need. And by spiritual I do not mean religious, although for many these two are entwined. By spiritual, I am referring to a need for self-fulfilment – what Abraham Maslow[1] would refer to as self-actualization – that will often combine with a desire to make a contribution or to be of service in the world. It is a deep-seated need that arises from within and goes beyond intellectual or emotional fulfilment.

Maslow says "what a man can be, he must be"[2] and describes self-actualization in terms of achieving all that one can. I believe the desire for purpose goes beyond mere achievement and requires a connection to a higher self, to God, to the Universe, to destiny, or any similar concept that draws you into a realm that is

---

[1] Maslow, A. (1954). *Motivation and personality*. New York, NY: Harper.
[2] Ibid. pp 91.

greater than yourself. When I refer to *mere* achievement, I don't mean to say that achievements are not things to attain to; en route to achieving purpose we may complete a university degree, travel overseas, win an art competition, get married, get published in a prestigious journal, have a baby, and much more... all achievements that may bring satisfaction and pride. Such achievements may or may not bring with them a sense of purpose though, or they may bring a greater or lesser sense of purpose.

Possibly, once you have come to this idea of needing a purpose, you may feel this as quite an urgency. You may even feel frustrated or depressed at not having a purpose or not being able to figure out what your purpose is. **Definitely do everything you can to keep anxiety or frustration or depression from creeping in; none of these things will help you in uncovering your purpose, and indeed they will act as obstacles.**

Having a purpose though is not at all the same as finding a cause. Some people *will* find a cause to dedicate their life to; as often as not their motivation will spring from a personal tragedy or experience that compels them toward that end. Purpose, though, has much more to do with the ways we interact with the world around us, than in finding some particular organisation or issue to commit to.

There is no doubt in my mind that each of us as human beings has a purpose. I've not always been without doubt, but mostly I can say I've courted my doubts with a view to questioning my beliefs and where I've got to in my understanding; something I've tried to do throughout my life. I don't hold firmly to my beliefs in the sense that they define me; it is more the case that I have become aware of certain truths, and then only because my limited human senses grasp some small part of something far more complex than my tiny mind can know in full. I think this is the nature of much of what we think of as universal truths; some people with one view see one part of it and some people see some other part, and the groups can argue black and blue for generations because they think their limited minds have grasped the whole truth when actually this is very rare. **Those that have a larger view of any particular truth never fight about it.** So in this regard I don't have beliefs so much as I have some things I've seen and understood. Because my experience of the world and of learning has been reasonably broad and open, I believe I have a reasonably useful view that's worth sharing; feel free to take from it whatever works for you and discard that which doesn't.

This book has emerged from several areas of research and points of learning, and in large part from my experiences teaching, talking to and coaching others in the pursuit of their purpose over several years. My own pursuit of purpose has been a journey of many years, aided by the instruction I've received from coaches and spiritual teachers around the world. This is not everything there is to know about purpose, but it's a worthwhile amount of useful knowledge with some structure applied. Once this makes sense and you have absorbed this into your understanding, there will be more, so much more.

Throughout the book I will use the terms God, the Universe, the Divine, Energy, Source, the Light and other such terms; and they are used, from my perspective, more or less interchangeably. If one of these terms doesn't sit well with you for whatever reason, feel free to replace it with your own, or you could just not fuss about it too much and recognise that they are all just words to describe the one great Essence that animates all of life. When people have said to me *I don't believe in God*, I would often somewhat facetiously say *Poor God.* Others I know would say *well, God believes in you.* Mostly now I find it a pointless discussion; they are words and they are all lacking in some way in their ability to convey this extraordinary truth.

My experience in teaching and coaching on the topic of purpose has almost exclusively been with people who are definitely seeking to make a positive contribution to the world, to bring something of Light and beauty into others' lives. The term *Lightbearer* has been used to describe these people who are to all intents and purposes entirely ordinary. They are not gurus or great spiritual teachers, although some may become this. They are people with some talent (perhaps as yet unexplored and undeveloped), with a desire to be of service, with a need for meaning and Light in their own lives, albeit that for many that may just be some vague and undefined notion. There are millions of these people; they generally feel things deeply, and it seems to me that a lot more than half of them are women. They are the future of humanity, and they are seeking purpose and meaning, sometimes desperately. Many of them are youth, who find much of modern life, with all its cruelty and superficiality, a burden. They are rarely supported in their school system to explore the world in a way that suits their view of it, and sadly they are often not supported by their parents either in a manner conducive to their soulful development; and we know too well some of the downsides of this lack of support, in the alarming statistics of substance abuse, mental illness and suicide.

The widespread need to understand purpose seems more recent – a part of some new era that is exploding with information about new ways of living and experiencing the world and connecting with the Divine. While any one Faith or philosophy may be deeply fulfilling for any of its adherents, **no religion or body of learning has exclusive rights to the recipe for the good life**, and indeed much of new and popular learning has emerged from spiritual teachers wholly unaligned with a particular group. There is much to be gleaned; I hope this small contribution assists your journey.

1 You Have a Purpose

The idea that each of us has a purpose has to be considered a spiritual idea. By this I don't mean 'religious', although for many their religious experience will almost certainly lend weight to their desire for purpose. And beyond religion, I don't necessarily even mean a belief in God, with or without any accompanying religion, although such a belief will also almost certainly give meaning to the need for, and belief in, purpose.

We have a spiritual part to ourselves, just as we have physical, mental, social, sexual and emotional parts, and they have different needs that are met in different ways. Our spiritual Self desires several things; it desires connection with Source, with the Divine; it requires spiritual sustenance; and it desires purpose. It is where our desire for purpose comes from. Of course our mental and emotional selves also want a degree of fulfilment in our work, but the real pull – the deep-seated need for purpose that we feel within us – is more than a need for some kind of emotional or mental satisfaction, and this is very plain and obvious to us when we feel that need for purpose. We experience that desire from the level of soul. Soul is the semantic understanding we have of our spiritual Self, just as Mind is the manifestation of our mental self (and we even think of it as being in our brain), and Heart is the manifestation of our emotional self (that we even think of often as our actual heart in our chest). We don't need to give religious meaning to the idea of Soul. If you want to then by all means, but

I'm trying to explain these concepts in a way that goes beyond religion, or our limited understanding of the Divine, in particular for those who prefer not to think in these terms or who have even rejected these concepts for whatever reason. It doesn't matter if you have a belief in God, or some other thing like that, or not; it's not a prerequisite for having a spiritual view of the world or having a spiritual experience, nor must you understand purpose as arising from a spiritual self as such – perhaps you prefer to think of your purposeful self – no matter. If you are here and reading this, then we are mostly on the same page together and you are looking to reveal and live a more purposeful life.

There are many facets to our purpose (although some I'm sure are beyond our meagre comprehension), and to give life to our purpose it is worthwhile exploring and understanding these different facets. Life is not charted for any of us, at least not in any very obvious manner, and if we can foresee its different parts we will certainly make an easier journey of it. We don't come into this world with a set of maps, but we have the extraordinary good fortune in this era in which we all currently live to have buckets and buckets of guidance in the form of thousands upon thousands of coaches, spiritual teachers, and academic researchers all over the world. Many of these have achieved levels of personal development and public notoriety in their own journey, such that their messages and teachings are shared broadly across the globe and they are leaders in assisting humanity in its current period of awakening. The Dalai Lama, Ekhart Tolle, Pema Chödrön, Neale

Donald Walsch, Deepak Chopra, Esther Hicks. Even Oprah has taken a significant role in providing a global level of visibility to many of these teachers. There are a myriad parts to play in this magnificent drama of opening ourselves and humanity to an exploration of the Universe.

Perhaps you too want to be some kind of spiritual teacher or coach, to contribute to advancing humanity in some way that has to do with spreading Light. If so, then like me you have probably also thought *well I'll never be a Neale Walsch or a Deepak or...,* and you will have already cut your nose off to spite your face. **It's not uncommon among those of us searching for our purpose that we're prepared to knock ourselves before we've barely started.** Consider the possibility that you can in fact be anything you want to be. I had a young woman in one of my classes once who wanted to be the first woman on Mars. Truly. That was her goal and she was sticking to it. She loved having that goal and it defined her in so many ways. She was very *alive* with her purpose. It was wonderful!

Believe anything is possible.

Wherever you think your purpose journey may take you, the very least you can do for *yourself* is believe anything is possible. What is the point of not being on your own side? Few if any people are born with a predetermined destiny for outrageous success and notoriety; perhaps some were born with some special opportunities, but just as many that were born with such opportunities took no advantage of them, and a myriad others reached dizzying heights with no leg up. Which is also a good time to mention that there's not a lot of value in comparing yourself to others. Life *is* a journey, and we're all at different points in it; one person may look as though they're further along, but they may well have some extraordinary obstacle they're dealing with that you cannot even see because you're not where they are. Our lives have depth and breadth of infinite complexity; it's best to focus on your own most of all and not try to analyse others' too closely.

By the same token, this is *your* journey and not someone else's. No one else can define your purpose for you. Many may assist you to see clearly and advise you along the way, but by its very definition, your purpose is only revealed to you, may only make sense to you, and can only be lived by you. When we have no clue where to begin, of course we seek others' input and suggestions, and hopefully those that know us well can be both insightful as well as objective.

It may be difficult to avoid the insistence of key influencers in our life, notably our parents, in wanting us to take a specific direction. My children's father and I both spent many years at university and have a mostly positive view of our academic experience. Our eldest child though dropped out of high school, deciding to become a stand-up comic, a journey that will in all likelihood take many years from which to even create a basic living. He is so alive with this purpose that I find it impossible not to be excited for him in his journey, not to mention that our home is alive with humour all the time. I do everything I can to support him on his unique path.

If family members are disapproving of your journey, that is *their* journey. It's not easy in those kinds of circumstances, but you must go your own way, and hopefully at some point your family will be able to see how important this is for you. Bless you.

2 Your Unchanging Purpose

Perhaps you have begun your journey of purpose with a desire also to grasp *the meaning of life*. This is another way of describing a similar part of our journey. Take a walk with me through a discussion on meaning and purpose. It's a bit of a windy road; bear with me.

There is the question of *the* meaning of life, and then there is a trailer-load of *meanings* of life, which is to say, all the many understandings we gain from life; the lessons we pick up along the way. The lessons may be things like:

There is almost nothing that's worth your integrity.

Don't lose something worthwhile because of something that's not.

Awful things can happen but sometimes those things save you.

There are greater and lesser lessons, but the main thing about lessons – the main lesson about lessons – is that **there is *always* a lesson to be learned**. Life is one long series of them, and we are doomed to repeat the ones we don't, can't or refuse to learn.

The meaning of life is simple: to live a life of purpose. I believe in an additional primary meaning of life, which is *to know and love God.* For me this is all but identical to *living a life of purpose.* God doesn't need me to love God for God's sake; God's perfectly fine with or without my attention. But if I believe God to be the Source of all Virtue, the Source of all our most deeply valued human characteristics – love, kindness, generosity, respect, creativity, honesty, peace... - then *to know and love God* becomes identical with *living a life of purpose,* since there is no *living a life of purpose* without simultaneously and inherently developing our own highest human qualities.

Let me divert to talking about God before those who have no such belief completely freak out at what I'm saying.

You don't have to believe in God, or anything similar, in order to be happy. Please allow me to express something I think is very important: your disbelief in God or any such thing is not something you should attempt to prove to yourself or others by putting others' beliefs in God down. Criticising others' beliefs is not an appropriate way to feel confident about our own; a bit like saying someone's ugly doesn't make you prettier, or pointing out that someone's wrong doesn't make you right. Hang in here while I try not to prove God either.

Similarly, if you believe in a *Higher Power*, or the *Power of Nature*, or *the Universe* or *Energy*, then it's better not to go on about how you don't believe in

God but you do believe in whatever it is. These really are all the same, and we don't do ourselves any favours by professing our dislike or disbelief in one way of describing the Divine over another. Few if any people that believe in God believe in an old man with a long white beard sitting on a cloud. Most in fact believe in an unseen, all-knowing, all-powerful force that is the same as your Higher Power, Universe, or Energy, so my personal view is that folks ought to give God a break. On the other hand, I also like to refer to the Divine, Source, the Universe and Energy.

At any rate you'll gather that I believe in God. I believe, by definition, there's only one God, although I notice a lot of people like to make God in their own image, and they give God all kinds of personal biases and prejudices, especially against religions that aren't their own. God doesn't have any of these biases and prejudices, nor does God belong to any religion, nor in fact did God create any of these religions, although I do believe God had a hand in providing us with different leading lights to help guide us, in the form of the Buddha, the Christ, the Prophet, and others. Sadly we have little in the way of actual words from those great prophets' own mouths, and instead we have a great deal of imagery, fantasy and metaphor from their followers, which has often served to strangle basic human freedoms and real spiritual development. I do not believe any of the negative outcomes of these religions or belief in their prophets (most particularly violent extremism), is the fault of the religion or the prophet. Abuse of power is evidenced in every walk of life and is one of the greatest of human failings. I am not a defender of such abuse, but nor am I interested in the abuse of religion that occurs either by those holding high rank within it who abuse their station, or by those who cannot differentiate between what is good and what is bad. The oft-expressed view that there is more murder, war and mayhem done in the name of religion is patently not true to any student of the history of war, and is pure ignorance on the part of those who react to unwelcome proselytization (over-exuberant preaching and teaching) from those around them. I despise ignorance in fundamentalism and I have no regard for fundamentalism generally; its proponents of any Faith do themselves no good, and need to learn to mind their own backyards. However such characters are not generally representative of any Faith, in word or deed – they are generally just the loudest voice. In addition, I am not blind to the risks of organised religion – they are in many respects no different from those of large corporations. Abuse of power comes easily when we have a lot of money and political favour, and as such have the ability to try to control how others view us.

So, back to God; or *Energy,* or *the Goddess,* or *Consciousness. God* by the way is gender neutral, and I do my best not to refer to *Him* ever, but again, since we don't have a gender neutral pronoun in English, we could just decide to get over ourselves on that one too. I understand though the great affirmational power for women of *the Goddess.* When I once considered the idea of God as female, it massively changed my view of myself at the time; that was many, many years ago, and I no longer think of God in terms of any gender.

I personally believe there is ample evidence for existence of a God-power, just because it is as plain as the nose on anyone's face that there is an animating force that underlies all living things, and that force is *almost* entirely beyond scientific reach and can largely only be explained with recourse to the Divine. You might want to refer to the *quantum* of things if you are a little versed in quantum physics, although this quantum also remains relatively unknowable in scientific terms, at least as yet. The best thing ever written on this, I believe, is *The Tao of Physics* by Fritjof Capra, one of the most important books I've ever read, and in continuous print since 1975. Capra followed this with *The Turning Point (1982), Uncommon Wisdom* (1988), *The Web of Life* (1996) and *The Hidden Connections* (2002). He is an Austrian-born American physicist and a faculty member at UC Berkley, among others. I cannot recommend his writing enough.

Back to the meaning of life and what I believe is our *Unchanging Purpose*. If we believe fundamentally that we are spiritual beings lingering a while on this Earth, then we can easily see we have at least a dual purpose; one overarching one that attaches to our never-ending spiritual self, and one that has to do with our sojourn here in our physical bodies. The greater purpose is the never-ending one, and the lesser must undoubtedly contribute to it. **When we understand our limitless self and the purpose that attaches to it, this also changes our view of our purpose in this life – it will tend to expand it, and it will also enlarge our attention to the simple responsibilities we have to be kind, to love others, to forgive, to not**

judge, etc. Indeed, we may increasingly see these simple things *as* our purpose and understand that anything else we choose to do is simply an adjunct to those.

If none of this explanation of the Divine works for you, then please do stick simply with the idea that we have some spiritual Self that is something different from our emotional or mental Self that is the origin of our desire for purpose. Alternatively I hope your own beliefs will find some way to sit with what you'll read here. It is my intention to offer these thoughts independently of any particular views.

The unchanging element of our purpose is to develop virtue.

Simply, the unchanging element of our purpose is identical for all of us and it is to develop in the Virtues. Key virtues include love, forgiveness, tolerance, courage, kindness, and so on. I'll talk about the particular part some of these play in our purpose further on.

We all have virtues; we will have developed some to a high level, and others will be areas of weakness for us, requiring more attention. The brilliant Maya Angelou described **courage** as *the fundamental virtue for the development of all others*, and I think this has truth. Courage is our ability to go beyond our fears and do what needs doing regardless. If we are afraid to forgive, or if our societal norm is to hate those who may have harmed us and to never forgive, then it will most certainly take courage to face the deep need of all of humanity and our own selves to develop forgiveness. **Developing any part of our personal self generally requires courage**, since it most often requires us to look at those parts of ourself that are lacking in some way, that we don't like, and that we are very often embarrassed and afraid to admit.

I've been hugely judgmental in my life. I'm judgmental in a certain way; I judge those who are prejudiced or bigoted against others who are different in some way from themselves. Perhaps those others are a different skin colour, a different religion, a proponent of different politics, a different sexual orientation, or a different gender. It is a part of our growth and expansion as people that when we face our own prejudices and move on from them, then for a while we can judge others still having those prejudices as lacking. Or when our experience of the world expands such that we see the ugliness of prejudice around us, then as we aim to stand up for those suffering the yoke of prejudice, we judge its perpetrators as less, as ignorant, as stupid, as hateful. Whilst it is good that we may have moved to a higher level of understanding and appreciation of difference and diversity, there is still no value in judging even those who have not understood and appreciated the value of others' uniqueness. It truly is just another level of judgment. When one prides oneself on one's tolerance and on one's appreciation for diversity, it is quite a wake-up call to discover that in fact one is still operating with an extraordinary level of judgement.

When I realised that was where I was at I felt embarrassed, indignant, and ashamed to have it pointed out to me; generally all good signs one needs to face something. I've found though that it's best to take a deep breath, feel humbled, maybe even express a few expletives at one's frustration with oneself if that is your way, and then look for ways to let go of whatever that thing is that's got its claws in you. In particular, to understand the flipside of that judgement, which you may be surprised to know boils down to a lack of love. Not that I wasn't loving – I'm very loving – but I didn't hold any love for those who practiced intolerance. I had no place in my heart for them. Nor did I want to at first, either. But I worked on it.

To remove judgement and intolerance, open your heart more.

Courage comes in facing our weaknesses, our flaws, our limitations – we all have them. Our journey proceeds as we respond little by little to those flaws and develop some new strength, some new virtue, to replace them. The simple answer to judgement and intolerance is to open your heart more. For me this came daily in meditation, and in connecting to and feeling the expansion of my own heart, and to trying on the idea that I really could love everyone unconditionally.

Trying on ideas is great. We can try them on like we're trying on a new coat in a store. We don't have to buy; we're just putting something on and seeing what it feels like. At a certain point this metaphor fails though, because of course if we don't feel comfortable in the new coat we won't buy it, whereas all new ideas can feel uncomfortable at first and that's not necessarily a sign we shouldn't buy them. Our biggest discomfort comes with our greatest shame and our greatest intolerance.

Let's take forgiveness. And let's take something that's typically very hard to forgive – the kind of thing we see in the news – think of actual real people if you can: a terrorist bomber, a serial killer of children, a brutal rapist; and then let's also take that politician or political party you hate; and while we're at it, let's also take that person at your work that makes your life hell or that you just can't stand because they got the promotion you deserved, and that ex-partner that cheated on you, and your mother who drank herself to death and made your childhood a misery, or your equivalents of these people in your life. You might be wondering how this has anything to do with your purpose; we're coming to that.

How do you feel when you think about these people? If you've not mastered forgiveness, you won't be feeling too good. You'll have a lot of anger, and you'll want to direct that anger at those figures, even if they're not around anymore for you to direct that anger at. (Maybe they haven't been around for years.)

Most of us haven't grown up with a very good understanding of forgiveness, except perhaps within religious settings, some of which have sadly put people off by the often narrow, prejudiced, oppressive practices prescribed by the leaders of some parts of religion.

I had always understood forgiveness as a generosity I didn't have much intention of giving to those who had harmed me (or who I believed had harmed me). Why should I? Why indeed should I forgive the paedophile, the rapist, the murderer, the war-monger, the chauvinist, the abuser, the wife-beater? Why should anyone forgive such atrocities? For the simple reason that if you don't you impede your own spiritual and purposeful journey in this life.

Anger serves no purpose.

There are multiple layers to understanding forgiveness and developing this virtue within yourself. One of the first to understand is that your anger serves no purpose: it offers nothing good or positive; indeed it causes you harm, emotionally and physically. At another level we learn that anyone's actions, including our own, are only the result of what we know at any given point. And by *know*, I mean the sum of our responses beyond what we understand to be right and wrong. But let's just stick with how anger harms us.

A second very important reason to forgive is that as long as we do not, that person (if it's a person) has a hold on us that brings out our anger, that leaves us bitter, that prevents us from experiencing love and joy. Do you really want them to continue to cause that reaction in you? Do you really want to allow them that hold over you? To prevent your happiness and joy?

Forgiveness – and letting go of our anger – doesn't necessarily mean we are letting them off the hook for doing something wrong; it means we're letting go of that event and the hurt surrounding it, and we're not going to allow it to continue to dictate how we feel.

If we understand purpose as a spiritual need, if we understand that a part of our purpose is to develop our virtues, if we understand that what is spiritual and what is virtuous stem fundamentally from the Divine, then quite simply we cloud our connection to that Source when we express anything that is not an expression of the Divine, and thus either our purpose remains unclear or we remain unable to express our purpose in our daily lives.

So we *must* forgive.

We must forgive for an array of important reasons, but at the very least we must forgive because not to causes us harm and blocks our purpose.

You cannot know what peace lies on the other side of forgiveness if you haven't tried it. There is certainly nothing good going on for you by holding onto the anger and anguish someone else has caused you.

The beautiful reward of forgiveness is that we allow more love in our lives. Once you experience that you will probably kick yourself for hanging on to your anger for as long as you did. Oh, and don't waste time and energy beating yourself up that you have been holding onto it as long as you have – that doesn't serve you either; it's just another lesson, and life is all about lessons.

A wonderful source of knowledge on the Virtues is *The Virtues Project* at www.virtuesproject.com. *The Virtue Project* lists 52 virtues, taken from a study of several hundred that emerge from an array of world scriptures and philosophies. This is a wonderful starting point for establishing, very simply, your own areas for particular development; it's also an excellent teaching tool for children.

In this particular time we live in – one of much turmoil – certain Virtues stand out as especially requiring our attention, as humankind, and those are **Courage, Forgiveness, Gratitude, Tolerance, Joyfulness and Service**. Just as the need for purpose is also part of this current era, so too is mastery of these particular virtues; they go hand-in-hand with the discovery and unfolding of our purpose.

Courage – Famous thinkers (Aristotle[3], Maya Angelou,[4] C.S. Lewis[5]) have described courage as the foundation of all the virtues. In my experience, when we're faced with having to change, let go of stubborn attitudes, and adopt more mature behaviours, it

---

[3] "You will never do anything in this world without courage. It is the greatest quality of the mind next to honour."

[4] "Without courage, we cannot practice any other virtue with consistency. We can't be kind, true, merciful, generous, or honest."

[5] "Courage is not simply one of the virtues, but the form of every virtue at the testing point."

generally requires courage. Forgiveness doesn't always come easily, not least when we feel especially wronged. It takes courage to understand its special value and give it life. It takes courage to admit *we* are wrong and discard outdated ideas in favour of tolerance. It takes courage to express our gratitude for a situation we're not enjoying because there is a lesson to be acquired from it. It can also take courage to pursue our purpose in the face of many obstacles. Indeed, it takes courage to have faith, in ourselves, in others, in Divine intention. We definitely know it takes courage to stand up for what's right: that our children's education is more important to us than nuclear arms, that providing basic necessities for the homeless is more important than a tax break for the wealthy, and so on. It takes courage to walk away from relationships, situations and jobs that cause us turmoil and prevent us from achieving our purpose.

Courage is a foundation for change.

How to achieve courage? Like anything else it is simply practice; stepping outside your comfort zone, specifically doing something *because* it frightens you, even if just a little, trying something new, experimenting, going on adventures, speaking up – there are a myriad ways to get in shape and the regular exercise of courage maintains your strength in this virtue.

Forgiveness – People are starting to understand what it really means to forgive. It doesn't mean that you're excusing someone for past wrongs, but it does mean you're no longer going to allow those wrongs to rule your life. Karma and/or the justice system will take care of whatever punishment someone ought to meet – that's rarely our prerogative to decide. Forgiveness means that you let go of your anger, hate or bitterness towards another, because holding on to those feelings only hurts *you.* We think if we hold onto our hurt and stay angry at someone that they'll somehow figure out the error of their ways and humbly apologise; this is rare and we only do ourselves further harm waiting for an apology that's never going to come.

One personal slight can ruin our whole day because, and *only because*, we hold onto it. We think about what we could have said differently, how we're going to get even, how rude that person was, how impatient they were pushing in, what an arsehole someone is because of whatever.

Why do you care?! It generally has absolutely nothing to do with you. Let it go.

Once again it's about practice. Start by letting go of those small personal slights that come our way every day – the car that pushed in front of you, the grumpy shop assistant, the person who talked as though you weren't there. Myself, I say that line from the movie *Madagascar* in my head: *Just smile and wave.* It works wonders. The instant you are literally able to put a smile on your face in response to such things, the instant the anger load lightens and even disappears completely... that's Grace. Grace in action.

Graduate to the harder ones: the relative you're not speaking to because they didn't invite you to something; the parent or sibling you're estranged from because why? We do of course make sensible decisions often in estranging ourselves from toxic people in our lives, but we should never close the door to the possibility of someone else's personal growth. **We can certainly love people from afar, but there is no point continuing to be angry at them from afar as well.**

Gratitude – There's a lot of new age talk these days about the value of being grateful, although gratitude has had a place at the heart of every religious and mystical tradition since time began. It's not always easy to understand why gratitude is so vital though. Certainly this means so much more than saying your *please*s and *thank you*s.

If we can learn to see every situation we find ourselves in, everything that occurs to us, as an opportunity to learn and grow, then we must be grateful for those situations, even the ones that seem harsh, or not especially desirable, at the time.

Lost love teaches us to deal with sorrow, heal, and love anew. When we missed out on the job we wanted so much and thought was ours, we learn perhaps there is something better waiting, or that we must acquire new skills to meet that particular demand.

I certainly often find it very hard to accept that the Universe's timing is better than mine. On the flipside though, as I express my gratitude more and more for the things I *do* have in my life, I simultaneously experience more peace with where I'm at right now, more trust in what the Universe has in store for me, and more happiness and greater abundance. As I've learned to express my gratitude, I'm less unhappy with the shape of my body, with the size of my bank balance, and I'm in much less of a hurry to get where I want to go – because I'm happy right here, right now. And I might add that the happier I am, the more my purpose unfolds before me.

Tolerance – Tolerance has a bit of a bad rap these days, since sadly the word has been misappropriated over time to mean *putting up with*, which reeks of superiority. In reality, tolerance has to do with living in peace with those of different beliefs and values, and it has far more positive connotations than it's been allowed to have more recently. Those self-righteously bent on intolerance – although they might not necessarily consider themselves so – would then add that they won't respect the beliefs of those who commit atrocities in the name of God. Which is not what tolerance is about. And then you start this whole big circular thing with the self-righteous Intolerant who refuse to forgive, who prefer to judge, and who generally seem to me to live in fear in their very homogeneous lives. Was that a judgement? Probably. I'm not perfect at this yet.

Be the change.

The thing that makes tolerance so important to this particular time we live in, is that our diversity is greater than it's ever been and with it our lack of tolerance. **Our primal self is wired for caution, and every difference presented to us can automatically alert subconscious warning systems – fear – unless we either *consciously* override them, or over time we re-condition our automatic response to one of openness and acceptance.** The way we override them is – again – by practice; practice of diversity and difference, and practice of loving all others. Expose yourself to the world! Let your heart, mind and soul be open to the reality of the Divine that exists in everyone regardless of their beliefs. And if their beliefs lead them towards destruction, it is not their religious Faith that has taught them this since none do teach this, but their own and others' misguidance and lack of education on the reality of truly living with purpose. We do actually have to *be the change* we want to see in the world. Our very best way to live is with love, respect, tolerance, and an appreciation for the Divine in others, regardless of how they choose to live their lives. That's what *being* the change means.

Joyfulness – Joy is something more than happiness. It's a level of happiness that engulfs your soul as well as your heart. The energy of joy is that much bigger than happiness that it's almost impossible not to be lifted up by the presence of someone experiencing it. **Joy is a door opening to the Divine, to God, to the Universe. Joy is the flow of Spirit within us. It is so powerful that it can heal our bodies and soften our hearts at the same time. It is the manifestation of love and has the power to change the world.**

Joy is the *spiritual* manifestation of happiness; it's what the spiritual part of our self in action looks like. I believe happiness is a manifestation of emotional health and joy emerges from spiritual well-being. Most of us have experienced joy, perhaps a little, perhaps a lot, perhaps momentarily. We're often able to experience joy in nature, watching a sunset or looking at the night sky; perhaps at the birth of a child or from the affections of a favourite pet; perhaps being in the presence of art, or in practising our own art. The more you experience joy, the more you invite the Divine into your life, the happier you will be. Joy feeds happiness and it feeds health. It is generally accompanied by a sense of wonder and beauty, and often the recognition of something greater than ourselves. We bring joy into our lives with our connection to the spiritual, and as we practise this we are able to hold onto joy for longer and longer periods. With joy, what we touch leads to success. With joy, we impact the world and everyone around us for the better.

Service – To quote Burmese activist Aung Sun Suu Kyi: *If you're feeling helpless, help someone.* When we're very low and we really want someone to rescue *us*, and even though it can feel like the most gargantuan task to get up and get out the door and go do something, it *is* amazingly powerful to go help someone else. We can thrill from the energy of having made someone else's life better.

Many years ago my husband attended a conference at Maryland University and stayed briefly in Washington DC en route. He had never been there before and was not a particularly confident traveller. For anyone travelling for the first time alone from

New Zealand to any one of the world's largest cities, the experience can be overwhelming. One of the most striking and disturbing sights in the U.S. is that of the homeless, which is not so apparent here. My husband wandered out from his hotel one day, and at some point began chatting to a homeless man, discovering that he was employed but just couldn't get enough ahead to afford somewhere to live. To cut a long story short, my husband took this man for a meal, and then at the man's request allowed him to come up to his hotel room and take a shower, at the end of which he went on his way, along with I think it was $100 or so cash my husband gave him. Soon after this my husband rang me at home in New Zealand – I recall it was the middle of the night – exhilarated at having taken a bit of a gamble and helped this man out as he had. He was literally on a high. He's a smart man – some may think otherwise after reading this – and he'd chatted with this guy, summed up his character, decided the man wasn't going to murder him in his hotel room, and that it was in his power to make a difference, however small. It felt enormous to my husband, and I've no doubt the man felt some positive faith in humanity after the experience too. I hasten to add that another friend of ours *was* murdered in his own home by someone he'd also brought home to help in a similar fashion, so I do recommend great care. The point though is that we gain an extraordinary reward for our service to others, particularly to the extent of its selflessness. It's an extraordinary little miracle that our selfless service generates love, and indeed joy, within *us*.

Our commitment to the Virtues is thus two-fold: *one*, that it is a key aspect of our purpose to develop our human virtues; *the other*, that doing this in turn clarifies the other aspects of our purpose. Love is circular – the more we give, the more we get. All of the virtues are grounded in Love as the fundamental essence of the Divine. The more they grow in us, the more Light fills our world. The more we reduce the size of the walls we've created against the flow of Divine energy and Light, the more that Divine Light infiltrates our life, and the more Light we actually have in our life.

If you are not developing in the Virtues, your purpose will not be clear.

What's more, if we are not developing these virtues in ourselves, the reality of their absence in our lives – which necessarily means the presence of anger, hurt, judgement, ingratitude and/or unhappiness – acts as a block to furthering our purpose.

If we understand that a) our purpose is spiritual in nature, and b) that understanding our purpose is a spiritual process, then we necessarily block the flow of spirit in our lives if our hearts and minds are filled with the wrong kinds of fuel for the journey. The journey requires love, gratitude, forgiveness, and so on. **These are the oil and gas our purpose runs on.** The more we practise these virtues and others, the more we open our Soul, the more we let the Divine in, the clearer our purpose becomes.

This commitment to acquiring virtue is a key aspect of purpose, and remains so throughout our lives, although the particular virtues we are in need of developing at any particular time will change.

3 Your Changing Purpose

We all have our own unique reasons for being here, our own calling, the particular contribution we want to make to the world. We can have multiple purposes and changing purposes.

For many, there is a strong sense of purpose in parenting, which is not to say though that for everyone who is a parent that is a purpose. Many people become parents without it being a major factor in their purpose; which also doesn't mean they're not good parents – it's just that it's a different kind of drive for some, a deep-seated need, and a task providing a potentially very high level of satisfaction.

This then is the particular part of purpose that everyone is *most* looking for, most trying to figure out. In my observation and experience, you will find it more easily when you consider it alongside all the other elements of purpose.

Your purpose in this regard will likely be different at 45 than it was at 25, too. And that's great. It may even change from one year to the next; in fact if establishing and living your purpose are an especially large part of your life, as they have been mine, then you will probably also find that there is a refining of your purpose that continues all the time.

Another noticeable aspect of this part of purpose is that there may well be times when you feel so very, very clear about your purpose, and others where suddenly the whole thing becomes very blurry. There will likely be every shade of clarity and fuzziness in between as well. This is partly to do with the refining process, and partly because we are simply always changing. Sometimes when we are changing we can feel lost. If you are in a new place in your personal development – one you've not encountered before – then you may feel excited and energised by the adventure, or you may feel unsettled and lacking in confidence. New experiences bring both of those things, and with a lack of certainty can come a blurring of what you may even have felt was very clear just yesterday. This is normal and natural and is part of growing and changing.

We all have days that don't feel as positive and exciting as others; days where we may even feel a bit dark and even hopeless. We have days where nothing seems to go right, where everything is negative and everyone around us seems to be picking a fight. Maybe you've had several of these days in a row; *maybe* you've had weeks or even months of those days. And when it happens like that, it's very challenging to keep on the purpose ride, to stay open, and to accept.

I believe, aside from real clinical depression, which I'll address also, **there are three reasons we have days like this**. One is that they're a natural part of the rhythm and flow of change; one is that we haven't accepted that they're a natural part of the rhythm and flow of change, and so we've become stuck in it; and the third is a process by which the development of new and positive energy – mental, physical, emotional and spiritual – necessarily pushes old negative energy out, and we literally feel that old energy releasing when we are feeling down or having an off kind of a day.

If you're not clear, don't worry about it. Worrying about it will just ensure it stays unclear.

At any given time we don't necessarily know which one of these is reality, and it doesn't matter. The point is that at any time you are lacking clarity, don't worry about it. Don't think too much about it. *Know* that just as you've had clear days before today, you will have them again in the future. You don't have to analyse the *why* of everything, and you certainly need to avoid getting stuck in the doldrums. Take a very light, easy view of those days, even in the face of their seemingly inherent darkness and heaviness. You don't have to take those days seriously; in fact they're the ideal days to be being as silly and ridiculous as you possibly can be.

I'll talk more about our negative self-talk, and how to respond to that, later in the book, but for the purpose of this particular section, I want to say that to have total clarity all the time is not realistic, *and* if we are not having moments of lack of clarity then on the whole we are not growing and changing. **Fuzzy days are indicative of change; accept them.**

Finding your purpose for right now – the main thing you want to be doing with your life at this moment – is naturally a process of discovery. And sometimes it is a process of re-discovery, as we reacquaint ourselves with long-held dreams and desires.

Perhaps you are clear on what that thing is, but you haven't believed you have the means to breathe life into it yet. Or perhaps you have some ideas about what you'd like to be doing, but it's not wholly formed. Regardless, one thing you must experiment with is taking chances. Anything new will take some courage to pursue, and for many of us our dreams can be pretty radical in a lot of ways – maybe we really do need to give up the work we're doing now to live the life we've dreamed of; maybe the thing we want more than anything is not what our parents had in mind when they paid for our college education, maybe we really want to be an artist or a performer or a lightworker of some kind. The Universe seems to be calling a lot of people towards these kinds of radical shifts, and increasingly to creative pursuits of one kind or another. **To ignore that call is to beat yourself bloody inside.** If you resist the pull of your soul, you will very likely become anxious, depressed and even physically ill. Your dissatisfaction with what you are doing currently will become more pronounced and you will make yourself miserable.

Let me be clear though: we all have to do the things we have to do. We have to pay the rent, we have to put food on the table; we have to pay the school fees and the car insurance and and and… We have to get our kids to school and home again, we have to take care of our aging parents; we have to support our spouse's late college education. We have to do *all* these things.

But you must do something every day that puts *you* in the direction of *your* calling. If today is not the day for the giant leap into the unknown, it is most certainly still the day for some action or activity that advances you along that journey. You *can* write a book in an hour each night or early each morning, for the next year or two. You can read, you can study part-time, you can meet other people who do what you want to do, you can join internet groups, you can take internet courses, you can test the water with your art by writing a regular blog; there is always something that will move you in the direction of your dreams, if only little by little.

Never discount the idea also of taking big steps. There is almost always a way to satisfy the day-to-day requirements of living that still need to be met, the ones you feel you would sacrifice entirely by making any momentous change in direction. **I have never met anyone myself who courageously took a leap into the seeming unknown and then regretted it.** The Universe has a way of supporting us almost miraculously and instantaneously with the brave choices we make toward purpose.

One of our biggest fears though is not in being able to afford to make a financial change, but in **worrying what others will think**. This is particularly the case if we think our friends and family all live normal lives. I say *think*, since normal, as we all know, is a setting on the washing machine. People do some pretty interesting things these days. But still, we can be anxious about others' reactions, and indeed there may be strange looks from some of those closest to us. Only you can decide how much you will allow the reactions of others to affect you and your major life decisions.

There can be a fine line too between how we think others' view of us, and how we actually see ourselves. Sometimes the excuse of what others may think is just that, an excuse. The harshest judgement of all may well be coming from yourself. What will *you* think of you when you are no longer the old, perhaps dissatisfying, but yet familiar, image of yourself? Does it scare you? Are you going to feel uncomfortable as the status-less artist and no longer the successful lawyer? Loss of status can be even more uncomfortable than loss of income to many. But there can be no judgement either in seeking status or struggling to let it go. Not of others or of yourself. The idea that some have a certain status and others don't is a construct of the society we live in, and we cannot change that these measures are there, rightly or wrongly. The more confidence we have in a new role pursued, the less these constructs affect us.

I've always known there were other things I needed to be doing with my life, but my ego drew me first in the direction of an academic life, followed by a corporate one. In the first instance I needed to prove my mental acuity, and in the second I had status, power and money. Of course both offered a great many pluses that were more than just ego strokes, but ego played a big part just the same. And then to give them up! It doesn't come easily, that kind of change. It *didn't*. It took things blowing up in my face, several times, before I woke up to the damage some aspects of my life – and my ego – were causing me, and to cast them aside in favour of a radically different journey.

Would you still do what you do now if it didn't come with money, power, authority, or status?

You can test the extent of ego's relationship to what you are doing by hypothesising the absence of ego factors from your current work. Would you still want to be doing what you're doing now if it didn't pay so well, if it didn't come with power, authority, and status? Or alternately, if you could have the same money, authority and status that you have now, what would you rather be doing with your life?

The more you pursue purposefulness in your life, the more your purpose becomes clear to you. When you are young it may be very clear that to travel around the worlds with your friends is the right thing to be doing right now. Later it may be that to become a parent is something of great purpose for you. Later still – particularly when your children are reaching their teens and leaving home – you may develop other desires. At each point also, your thoughts and ideas about what purpose *is* will change. What is meaningful at 21 may be completely different at 50, or it may be that at 50 you return to the ideals of your youth.

I don't recommend getting to hung up on the idea that you have a singular purpose in life and that you must find it. Whilst it may be the case that you do have a singular purpose, it will surely be the case that it is given best effect by following your instincts at each particular point in your life. I don't believe I operated with anywhere near the purposefulness at 21 that I do now, but I can look back at the things I did in my 20s and 30s and see the contribution they still made to what I'm doing now in my 50s.

You can have multiple purposes and you can have more than one purpose going on at the same time. And those multiple purposes may be complementary or they may be very different. Only you can know when you are living aligned with your purpose, just as only you can know when some new direction is calling you.

4 Your Purpose to Make a Difference

What does it mean *to make a difference?* And why is *making a difference* an essential component of your life's purpose?

For a start, *making a difference* doesn't necessarily mean you have to look after sick people, dig latrines in Africa, give away all you own, work for nothing, never work for a corporation or any kind of for-profit venture, grow your own vegetables, use only public transport, or volunteer a hundred hours a week in your community. It can though mean any of those things if that is where you have some passion or commitment.

Making a difference is a human obligation to give more than you take – or at least to *do no harm* – and only you can take the measure of this, which correspondingly means that you cannot presume to take the measure of another's contribution, much as we are all tempted to.

There is a view that says that we are here to take as much as we can and that we have no obligation to give anything to anyone if we don't wish to. It is a difficult proposition to argue against with anyone who believes this, and it's not so easy to even prove to oneself that this cannot be so. It's difficult to argue, because the argument rests entirely on the belief that it's just not so.

This is not to say though that we cannot take much pleasure from life; indeed, we should try to take as much pleasure, joy, happiness and adventure as we can, albeit that it's rarely if ever something that should occur at the expense of others, their rights or their dignity. Life *is* an adventure. When we experience joy and happiness, we imbue our own lives and the lives of those around us with those things.

Generally those seeking purpose *are* looking to *make a difference* as well, but what I'm saying here is that **your purpose *is* to make a difference**. It doesn't even seem rational to have the idea of a purpose *without* also holding to the view that one must make a difference.

To be purposeful is by definition to make some change. And if our view of purpose has some kind of spiritual basis, then it cannot be to make anything less than positive change, and indeed to make change in the direction of improving the human condition and experience.

Some of us dream of changing the world in significant ways, and many of our contemporary idols are people whose contribution is vast: from Oprah to Eleanor Roosevelt; from Steve Jobs to Gandhi. As with clarifying our purpose, along the way to making a difference, we can feel frustrated that we're not there yet. Just as we may need to work in a less than fulfilling job to pave our way to the role we most want, we must also make as much difference as we can wherever we are.

Here is an extraordinary truth for those seeking to make a big difference: the more positive contribution we make in our daily lives with the people around us right now the greater the contribution we will be called on to make in the lives of more and more people.

The more you serve, the more you will be asked to serve.

Recently, a man sought my advice saying he had achieved enlightenment and wanted to write a book about it. I suggested he should teach whoever was around him to teach and if what he had to teach was good then someone would probably write the book for him. He replied saying no one believed him that he was enlightened, to which I responded that it didn't matter if he was enlightened or not, he should just teach whoever was around to teach. He replied several times trying to argue with me that he was indeed enlightened. I really wasn't interested in an argument with this man – I didn't know him – and so I didn't respond any further. The thing is, if you want the opportunity to serve more people, you must start by serving the people who are around you to serve now. The more you serve, the more you will be asked to serve. If you are seeking the opportunity to serve because your ego desires such privilege, you will not be given that opportunity; *or* you *will* be given that opportunity if only to show you how easily you will mess it up because your ego is in the way. Know your ego.

You may still be stuck wondering *how* you can serve the world in the pursuit of your particular purpose. A lot of people tell me they want to help others but they really don't know what to do to achieve that, what career to pursue, or how. Only you can answer that, but almost every role in existence does indeed serve some purpose – if it didn't, it would not be sustainable.

It is not only in your singular purpose that you will find the opportunity to make a positive difference in the world though. With every growth in your personal development of the virtues, with every step you take closer to the Light, you are impacting the world around you in a positive way.

Every positive thing you do impacts the world in a positive way.

I love the theory of the butterfly effect. I like it for its scientific value, as well as its more romantic value – it's a great thing to play with when you're an historical novelist.

The concept derives from the idea of the birth of a hurricane being contingent on whether or not a distant butterfly had flapped its wings several weeks earlier. Or to put it another way, who would think that a butterfly flapping its wings here in Wellington might cause a stampede of cattle in Wyoming? Who would think that the actions of one of us might tip the balance in favour of world peace? Who would think even that the *thoughts* of one of us would tip that balance?

But indeed they can.

(This, by the way, is one of the main premises of my novel *Angels in the Architecture,* if you've not already read it.)

When we replace thoughts of anger and irritation with thoughts of love and peacefulness, we contribute to a better world. Oddly, we can be much attached to our angry thoughts. It amazes me how I will insist on staying angry at someone I'm annoyed with, when just being nice, polite or kind would make me and them feel so much happier. I can offer no explanation as to this insanity of ours, whereby we insist on staying miserable; all I can say is that you must try to put that insistence gently to the side and attempt, however difficult, to be nice. We *have* to learn to do this with the people closest to us. Sometimes, amazingly, we can be more gracious with people we barely know than we can with those around us, but our obligation to put our best foot forward applies to everyone we meet.

Purposeful living *is* all about you, but it's also all about everyone else, especially those around you and the planet we live on. We are part of one great living organism, and just as taking care of our own mind, body and spirit helps the flow of purpose and purposeful living in our life, so too is this enhanced by our ability to contribute to the Earth's and humanity's health and well-being.

The Arts are one of the greatest contributions.

Many people that are now participating in this millennial shift to *make a difference*, aside from perhaps not being clear on *how* to do this, will often tell me that their real passion is to sing, write music, paint, or be engaged in some other art, and often this desire produces in them some notion that they're selfish to want to do this. I could not disagree more with the idea that to immerse oneself in one's art is selfish. There is hardly any greater contribution to the world than art in its many forms. Art of all kinds brings us joy, albeit that beauty is in the art of the beholder. I cannot imagine a world that had not produced van Gogh, Monet, Frida Kahlo, Mozart, Vivaldi or the Beatles. I paced my living room putting my infant son to sleep to very loud Beatles; I have nothing but joy from this memory. I love a road trip with Vivaldi's *Four Seasons* on the stereo. I have art on my walls produced, or given to me, by some of my best friends. I've stood in front of Monet's *Water Lilies* panels at the Museum of Modern Art in New York City, so blissed it brought tears to my eyes. I remember buying a children's story book about Monet's garden for a young friend; she was ten years old at the time and has dreamt of visiting Giverny her whole life. She recently went – twenty-four years later – with her own ten year old daughter and their photos have given me so much joy. My appreciation is not just in the beauty of these different forms of art, but in their meaning, in my understanding of what their authors were attempting to convey to their audiences. Such contributions can make as much difference to creating a positive, peaceful world as any other perhaps more obvious effort.

You make a difference when you raise your children with an awareness of the virtues, and when you support them to find their purpose. You make a difference by committing yourself to courtesy and respect even in the face of hostility. You make a difference when you recycle. You make a difference when you buy local, fresh, organic produce. Whilst I adore books, I have to say you make a difference having an e-reader and saving a tree or three in your own lifetime.

If, for you, your purpose does indeed stem from a firm commitment and connection to Spirit, then I can assure you Spirit cannot and will not guide you in the direction of anything less than *making a difference*. And if any concept of the Divine eludes your personal commitment to purpose, by the same token I would say to you that your own well-trained instincts will almost certainly not deceive you in the pursuit of your passion.

5 Assisting Others' Purpose

Some people, by virtue of their particular work, will have a lot more opportunity to assist others with fulfilling their purpose, but nonetheless it is incumbent on all of us to make this particular contribution where we can.

There are three main roles where we can help advance another's purpose: as a parent; as a coach, counsellor or therapist; and as a boss. I've been – I am – all of these.

Parenting is a challenge and far be it for me to advise any parent on how to raise their children, nor especially on how to guide one's children into one's learning, career, or purpose. I can only share my own experience and what I've come to believe about this vitally important role.

Firstly, I will say that I was most definitely very driven to become a parent, and I believe it has been a very definite purpose in my life. I adore my children, and we worried about their education before they were born. We didn't necessarily want our children to get to university, although we both had extensive university careers ourselves; I think we were most determined that they'd be happy, kind, aware of the world around them (especially its politics), have some idea of a spiritual life, and be able to figure out their path in life sooner than we had – we'd both dithered around figuring this out, albeit in different ways: I'd worked hard all my life whereas my children's father had mostly floated between unemployment and university. His ideal had been to have someone pay him to think – something he was very good at – eventually finding his niche as a government strategic policy analyst, primarily in the area of human rights and bio-ethics. Not knowing what to do with myself after finishing high school, my mother sent me on a secretarial course; I aced typing and shorthand, coming out top of my class and getting a series of office jobs for the next two or three years. My mother died around this time – I was 20 – and this devastated me. I somehow ended up wanting to become a nurse, as she had been, something I'd never in my life been interested in; a very Freudian type of response I realised eventually. I loved my nursing training, but nursing itself was never really my thing, so I left after a year in practice (although I *loved* operating theatre where I'd spend most of brief nursing career). I went into the medical industry selling surgical and cardiology equipment and stayed in this for ten years, ultimately running my own multi-million dollar company and employing several people. In the end this no longer served my need for something more purposeful; although I was at a loss to figure out what *more purposeful* meant to me. I went to university completing an undergraduate degree in philosophy and political science, and then taking on an Honours year in international law and international relations – I finished First Class – and a Masters in Business. I then spent several years in business, as a coach, consultant and CEO, much of which did a great deal to satisfy my bank balance and ego. But again I found myself out of touch with myself and my own purpose, having also managed to entirely wear myself out physically and emotionally, not once, but at least twice. I became decidedly disillusioned and let down with the lies and deceits of many people I had somehow found around me during this time. At another time in the future, I would recognise the lessons from these people and come to see them as some kind of blessing in my life; at the time I simply dipped out, wrote a novel, and focused on being a parent to my two now-teenagers, both of whom were suffering to some extent also from my somewhat ego-driven career and general absence.

My son, an extremely clever young man, had not been happy at school for a long time, although his experience improved marginally when he transferred from a rather Victorian uniform-bound, detention-focused high school, to one with a more contemporary view of the modern teenager. By this time the damage the school system was able to inflict had left him with little motivation to rise up and make the effort one more time. We like to say that school failed him, not the other way around. Halfway through his final year he announced he really had had enough and could not suffer through the final six months; he wanted to give up and become a comedian. Three years on, he is happy, focused, confident, charming and *extremely* funny, with a voice reminiscent of Ireland's Dylan Moran and a look like Ed Sheeran, although he'd like not to be known as the comedian that sounds like Dylan Moran and looks like Ed Sheeran.

Two years into my Teen Time Off, I decided I dearly wanted to take my daughter to see the world – she was intensely interested in other cultures, other languages, other food, other people; and whilst she was always a diligent student at school, I could see she was starting to feel the pressure of the inanity of it all too. Somehow we were both experiencing this simultaneous desire to see the world and so I focused on how I could create sufficient income to sustain us through several months of international travel. Initially we stayed relatively close to home, travelling to Australia for two months, before returning home and preparing for the US, UK and beyond. These next stops kept us going for five months, and I think we would have stayed longer if we could. In the end we really were running out of money. It changed my daughter's view of the world – she was 14 when we left and 15 when we returned. She became very clear through this period that **the most important thing for her to do in her life was follow her dreams** and her passions, which in the main were about becoming an artist.

Since then, she has had some strong views expressed to her by other members of her family about the value of university and perhaps a more conventional career, and this was done in such a way that she felt her choices were not being respected or valued. It seemed to me these were about those other people's unmet expectations in their own lives. I've no doubt they all love my daughter very much, but it was clear that they took a somewhat fear-based view of how one should live one's life, as well as adding other expectations that indeed failed to recognise not only her wishes but also her very real talent. She has navigated all this beautifully, sometimes with confidence and sometimes not so much, but always insisting on figuring out her own life plan.

Despite the very real challenges to succeed in their chosen careers, both my children have refused to be fearful and instead to believe in themselves, knowing that every artist was once an amateur.

I know I have contributed to their understanding of the inherent value in pursuing their dreams and passion, not least since I have been determined to do the same for some years now, making sure also that learning happiness, and developing my spiritual connection, have been requisite aspects of that dream.

I once heard Esther Hicks say that the sole responsibility of parenthood was to support our children to develop their connection with the Divine so that their own particular purpose became apparent to them. Of course we also do that by teaching what's right; for instance, when my children were young being kind was important, and they are very kind. Love – feeling it, bestowing it, learning it – is a key path to the Divine; indeed, love *is* the Divine, and the Divine is love; and so, to love our children – to bestow unconditional love upon them – is a simple and powerful means to them establishing for themselves what their purpose is. We mess that up though the minute we too strongly direct them into some particular path that we believe is important for their development, whether a particular education or a particular career. Even the latter part of high school, given its ability worldwide to suck the life out of our children, does not *have* to be a thing of pressure that we apply to our children. Whilst one hopes that the bulk of the high school system will one day leave the

Victorian era and step into the 21st century, its unwillingness or apathy or general inertia in this regard must not be the thing that knocks the notion of purpose from our children's lives, replacing it with some pressure to conform, to *get-a-job-any-job*, to become part of a soulless nine-to-five rat race.

Coaching or teaching or healing or actively having a role in helping others develop some part of themselves, gives one a unique opportunity to support clients' desire for purpose, even if they don't recognise that need or desire themselves.

At the root of any such help is an understanding of the different aspects of purpose I've talked about here, how to communicate these in ways that are meaningful to people, and how to continue to support people through their unfolding purpose. Depending on our age and life experience, our purpose can take years to become apparent, necessarily taking us through many self-imposed obstacles and the stories we've learned over decades to tell ourselves about our imagined limitations and imagined non-deservedness.

It has taken me a good few years to learn how to love myself and to believe that I'm deserving. I've been fortunate to have some wonderful coaches over the last several years who have taken me through various steps in self-discovery. I've always thought there was a certain triteness to the admonition to *love yourself first*, in the sense that I've seen it trotted out by coaches and healers and so on all over the place but never with any guidance on how on earth one does that! It's always reminded me of the thing our mothers told us before we went on dates or to parties: *just be yourself* – and I've always wondered what a ridiculous thing that is to say to a teenager. How many teenagers know what *being yourself* means?! They generally have few clues who they are yet and the idea of *be yourself* just adds additional pressure as far as I can tell.

So, yes, how on earth do you love yourself?

Constant and persistent practice.

We have this crazy idea that once we understand what a problem is and we *know* what we *should* be doing to fix it, that we've then got that thing nailed. We wouldn't know how to read music and then expect to play the piano – it takes *years* to learn to play the piano well. It will take you years to learn how to love yourself; and the older you are the longer it will take, not because you don't learn as fast but because you have to undo the habits of your lifetime.

Stop beating yourself up.
And stop beating yourself up for beating yourself up.
And stop beating yourself up for beating yourself up for beating yourself up.

It's not the focus of this book to teach you how to love yourself, but simply put you need to identify, halt and reverse all the many negative messages you give yourself, replacing them with positive ones; and as you're doing this, not to beat yourself up over your inability to be an expert at this task, nor beat yourself up for having beaten yourself up. Etcetera.

My most frequent coaching advice, generally with people who are looking for their purpose, is to work on halting their own negative voices, and to understand that all negativities act as a barrier to revealing their purpose. And then it's very much about supporting people to follow their passions, believe in themselves, and trust the Universe and its timing.

When you're **a Boss**, and especially if you're the business owner or the top boss, you're in a unique position to support people's development in this way.

Many times in my career as a business owner or CEO, I've had the opportunity to support employees in new and more meaningful (for them) directions.

Most business owners or leaders don't seem to consider this their role or responsibility, but if you take the view that you're here to support others in the discovery and development of their purpose too, then not only does this become your responsibility, but it also pays dividends in securing staff loyalty and commitment in many ways. People cannot be seen as a means to an end in any business; a business *is* its people and is an end in itself.

One of the things I've often discussed with staff at performance appraisal time is *what do you most want to do with your life?* And I follow this up by saying how I recognise that rarely do people stay in any one job for more than a few years. So whether it's a step up in your current business or the creation of opportunities for a staff member to mature into a new role in another business, I would prefer to help someone's career development as much as I can, within some sensible limits. Few of us get this opportunity – if you do, take it. When you're in a position to make a difference, make it.

Support people's purpose-driven choices.

There are other less complex, more day-to-day things we do to support others in their purpose. Show an interest in others' life and career decisions, support their choices, offer to assist when you can, be a sounding board for friends and family trying to figure out their path, and just be kind. Every one of us is having to make our own way. Sometimes a kind and caring word from a friend is gold.

6 Obstacles to Your Purpose

There are many obstacles to finding and living our purpose. The following are some of the main obstacles people mention:

- You don't know what your purpose is
- Other commitments are in the way
- You can't afford to pursue your purpose
- Ill-health or disability stand in your way
- You're afraid
- Your self-talk is all negative
- Judgment, guilt, shame, the past, forgiveness
- Lack of clarity

You don't know what your purpose is – It can be maddening to have a strong sense of desiring to live according to one's purpose and then to not know what that purpose is, either at all or more clearly. This maddening feeling can literally become an obstacle in itself as anything we experience negatively acts as a block to insight and inspiration. In addition, that frustration itself stems from that equally maddening desire we have to know everything instantly: *If I have a purpose I want to know what it is, right now, so I can get on with it!* It's like that funny meme: *Give me Enlightenment NOW, dammit!* It doesn't work like that. Our whole life is *about* a) *finding* our purpose, and then b) *living* it. Even when we've found it and we're living it, it still changes and swerves, and pitches this way and that. We have to let go of the need to get to the end of the journey, because it will only get us to the end of our life's journey – death – quicker, and not leave us feeling at all fulfilled. Whether you realise it or not, what you *really* want is to be *on* the journey, not at the end of it; at least not yet. And you *are* on the journey. Just reading this book means you're on the journey. You will have already gained so much insight just in the pages you've read so far; you are most definitely working on your purpose *right now!* And you will keep working on it, forever. That's the idea. So let go of the frustration and angst you have over your lack of clarity about the specific thing you need to be doing right now, because it's another obstacle in itself. When you hold on – and you may not think you're holding on, but you almost certainly are – to negative responses, you necessarily prevent positivity finding a way in, or at least you make it very difficult. **Positive energies of all kinds are very powerful and you can let them in and let them flow with ease just by letting go of the things that anger and frustrate you.** When you angst over not knowing your purpose, you're setting up an additional obstacle to that purpose revealing itself to you.

Other commitments are in the way – We all have commitments. We have to pay bills, put food on the table, and most especially take care of our children, and very often others who've become our responsibility also, such as elderly parents. We have to clean the house, do the dishes and mow the lawns.

I work twenty hours a week for a community care organisation responsible for supporting severely intellectually disabled clients; I have two teenagers, a house (with everything that entails), a dog, five Facebook pages and several other social media to make posts for every day, and I'm writing this book. As I speak. As I live and breathe. Oh and I go to the gym three or four times a week; in fact I just got back from the gym and sat down at my computer again. The dog is vying for my attention, and my son and his girlfriend are playing a loud computer game in the next room. The kitchen bench doesn't look the best but I never said I was perfect. Before I go to bed, I'll probably fold the washing that's in the dryer. Plus I'm 'on call' at the moment – 24/7 – once a month for a week, which means I'm likely not to have a full night's sleep, which I really don't like but it goes with the territory.

Don't make the excuse of not having enough time.

When my children were small – three and five – I took on a Masters degree at the same time as completing a full Honours year[6] at university. I was a single parent and super-organised. I got a First Class Honours,[7] which I was extremely proud of. And I am not wealthy; I make enough to live on. I am *extremely* happy with what I have, with my life and the people in it. I'm very grateful for all of it.

---

[6] Honours' is an English university practice that's basically a fourth year following a three-year undergraduate degree; it's considered post-graduate and it's also considered a harder university year than a Masters.

[7] An A-average earns a First Class Honours; followed by Second Class-First Division and Second Class-Second Division, and finally a Third Class which I guess is a C-average.

I don't watch television – I tend to binge watch several episodes of a favourite series via my computer. I do read – every day if I can, usually for at least an hour.

Having said all of that, a key factor of purpose is that it's what we do, arguably every moment of every day. If you are learning and growing and experiencing the world, then you are living purposefully. You don't *not* live with purpose all day until you find a spare half hour to live your purpose once a week!

In all my coaching experience I'm rarely able to accept someone's excuse of not having enough time; it's invariably just that: an excuse.

You can't afford to pursue your purpose – Almost every direction can be pursued without money; and there's almost always more money available than you think. I do realise how challenging the current financial climate is for many people; more and more people are just getting by or not even really managing that. The thought of new directions – whilst at heart desirable – just seems impossible, perhaps they even seem ridiculous or maybe you even feel they are irresponsible to consider when you have a family to support.

First of all, thinking about them – dreaming about them – is certainly not ridiculous or irresponsible. When you daydream about things you'd love to do – and especially if you do so with a view to them coming true (rather than just indulging them but all the while believing them impossible), you're creating an Energy around your goals that will attract their reality to you; you'll have ideas about how you *can* make them happen. It really is true that many of the most worthwhile things in life take time, maybe years, maybe decades. And anyway, what's the hurry? I don't believe the Universe/God expects us to fulfil our purpose the moment we reach adulthood. We may very well have to acquire many other skills before we seriously get to that part of our lives – who knows? The Journey takes us many places we hadn't expected.

Social media and entertainment media abound with stories of women and men who made their way from poverty to riches, from obscurity to fame, from ill-health to well-being, from deprivation to abundance, from ordinary to amazing, from unhappiness to joy, from victim to victor, or – as the song goes – *from misery to happiness today, uh-huh, uh-huh.* I'm on my way.

No matter what else you are doing, you can always be working on your goals in some way.

The moment we start to work on our goals in even the smallest way, more of our purpose will unfold before us – perhaps just a little at a time, but it will happen. You must not *not* be working on your goals, ever. *Even* if you don't really know what they are yet.

As with having enough time, we don't *not* live with purpose until we can afford it. And it may even be that having more wealth stands in the way of pursuing one's purpose. From time to time it's been my observation that the ability to create abundance has seemed a very specific skill someone has had to learn in the pursuit of their purpose.

There are *always* things we can do in the direction of our purpose when we think we don't have enough money to pursue our goals. There are *always* ways to make more money that don't compromise our values or our goals. We live in an era of the greatest ingenuity when it comes to making money. Despite the hardships many face, the world is awash with money, and with courage as a key foundation, and curiosity as a useful add-on, we can almost always find what we need, albeit that it may take time. In the meantime, there are always steps in pursuit of your goal that can be taken without money.

Ill-health or disability stands in your way – I have a lot to say on this topic, since I've experienced aspects of this myself, and also have many, many clients who have a physical or emotional ailment of some kind that's clearly acting as an obstacle to a happier, more purposeful life. I must also add here that not *all* ill-health or disability stands in the way; many people have achieved highly purposeful and happy lives despite their health or disability. So this section is really referring to those for whom their health or disability *is*, or feels like, an obstacle.

Our physical, emotional and spiritual
Selves do not operate in isolation from
each other.

Any physical, mental or emotional event or
condition that interrupts our daily rhythm and flow is
identical in its effect to negative thinking. If we are ill,
if we are angry, if we're suffering emotional hurt, if
we're exhausted, if we're *over-thinking* situations,
every one of these stands in the way of positivity,
happiness, satisfaction and the unfolding of our
purpose. Here we must understand that our physical,
emotional and spiritual Selves do not operate in
isolation from each other. They *always* impact each
other; the impact of one upon the other may be
lessened where those different parts of ourselves are
highly developed, and that is indeed *why* we must aim
to have all these different parts of our Self developed.

One of the greatest of emotional hurts is the death
of someone close to us. Regardless of any beliefs we
may have that our loved one has gone on to a better
place we feel these losses as if the world is turning
upside-down. My mother died when I was twenty and
it had that effect. I adored her and was very close to
her. Not being really quite an adult yet it was, and
remains, the most difficult loss of my life. I was very
angry through much of my twenties and probably
could have found some refuge in alcohol and drugs if
not for a firm stance against both. Simultaneously
though, my mother's death left me with the deepest
need to understand why we are here, what our purpose
is, and also where she had gone. I felt her influence

powerfully through my twenties and thirties and felt her presence in the midst of some later hardships also. She was an artist – a painter – and completed a vast array of her work in the last year of her life, knowing as she did at that time that she was indeed going to die. She had developed a breast lump when I was seventeen and this was misdiagnosed by the surgeon she consulted; back then mammograms weren't standard diagnostic tools. When the lump was suddenly bigger, she visited a different surgeon with the result that she then required a radical mastectomy, followed by radiotherapy and twelve months of chemotherapy. Back then – the early eighties – chemotherapy was even more horrendous than it is now; I remember nights where she experienced terrible nausea, retching and vomiting, and I – a teenager – had barely any idea how to process this. Her treatments ended and life seemed to return to normal for her for a while, until regular testing ultimately revealed liver metastases and she was given six months to live. She made it to twelve, in relatively good health ironically.

Constant negative emotional responses cause physical damage over time.

Anger, sadness, bitterness… these literally do break our heart. Anger damages our liver, which in turn reduces our energy levels. Sadness damages our kidneys, which in turn can give rise to depression. These are not the mental-physical connections standard medicine makes but virtually *every* other healing tradition describes these specific emotional-body connections. Over-consumption of alcohol and drugs – either recreational or prescribed – will undermine the functioning of our liver, the powerhouse for all other systems.

We cannot *avoid* much of the stress that appears in our lives. We cannot help that people we love die, we cannot always avoid conflict – and indeed we grow in other ways in our experiences around conflict; we never plan to break up with our partner but relationships don't always go the way we would wish and we can be left hurt and deflated. For women, pregnancy, birth and motherhood are *huge* stressors – ones we would generally not replace for anything, but they nonetheless take their toll on us in every way, especially physically. As many women do, I suffered ghastly morning sickness during pregnancy, and in my second pregnancy this was diabolical. I was bed-ridden for six weeks during the second part of my first trimester, vomiting several times a day. At one point my doctor took blood samples to measure my HCG (human chorionic gonadotrophin), high levels of which could indicate twins. My HCG was through the roof; I remember her phoning to tell me *You're not faking it, are you?* I tried various natural remedies, one of which included a Chinese herbalist who tested my *chi'i* – my life energy. She said I had none. I wasn't sure if that made me technically dead or what, but I sure didn't feel like I had much life energy either. It was reassuring of course to know that this is basically the result of having an extremely healthy placenta, and thus a very healthy baby. By my second trimester things improved, but the impact of the first trimester's ill health left its toll. In my third trimester I contracted cyto-megalovirus – similar to glandular fever – which left me again with no energy – I wanted nothing more than to lie down and sleep all the time. As I neared my due date, I feared I had *no* energy for childbirth and planned an elective caesarean, which did not sit well with me at all since I had planned another natural home birth. The virus though disappeared as quickly as it had arrived and all went according to the original plan, and I popped out a rosy, nine-pound daughter, Ruby.

Some will already be predicting what came next though. Two weeks after Ruby's birth, my *Third Day Blues* were still there and I was still weeping. I rang my best friend who also happened to be a midwife, and she told me I *probably have a little post-natal depression.* At this point I had no comprehension of the emotional-physical link to kidneys and liver; nor though was I of the view that I would be going anywhere near a doctor to treat my depression. I tried, not very successfully, to treat myself with natural remedies, and as you do when you have small children I just kept going. It wasn't until Ruby was around three years old that I decided perhaps medication was in order and a visit to my GP revealed I could tick all ten of the boxes on the questionnaire she gave me, including thoughts of suicide. So I found myself on a Prozac prescription, with two small children, newly separated, and undertaking a degree at university. Despite how it sounds, life was actually great. I wasn't keen to be on medication, although I was delighted to have lifted my mood and be feeling consistently happy for the first time in so long. Over the succeeding ten years I tried several times to take myself off the medication. I stress here that you must only ever do this under the supervision of your doctor, and never, ever go *cold turkey*, which is to say do *not* stop taking anti-depressant medication instantly; you should wean yourself off it.

Various events intervened – life does that – to both support and thwart my efforts to cure my depression. (Medication is not a cure; it simply alleviates symptoms and generally if you stop taking it – especially if you have a severe depression, which I did – the symptoms return. There is no conventional medical *cure* for depression.) Over time and with the help of some fabulous people I met along the way, I gained more understanding of the connection between my body, my mind and my spirit – really that there is no separation between them – and was able to heal each with the other. Challenging myself to take on larger roles in my career though, I came unstuck with the stress that appeared to come hand in hand with these. I travelled a great deal, I worked long hours; there was a great deal of pressure from many directions. In three successive roles I found myself working with and for people who were deceitful and/or bullying to an extreme, and the effects were not positive. It's extraordinarily difficult to maintain your composure, your life balance, your personal balance, and your own integrity when you're in the midst of dishonest situations. I found myself questioning my own integrity at every turn and judging myself harshly; assault on one's self from one's self is often unconscious and certainly the most dangerous since we believe ourselves more, at least at a subconscious level.

We can get *the blues* for any number of reasons, from any number of different mental and emotional antagonists. Clinically, for whatever reason, reduced levels of *serotonin* are one significant factor among many, many hormonal-level possibilities – and by *hormonal* I don't mean only those things that effect women more than men. The majority of our body's hormones are not gender-specific and there are hundreds – probably thousands – of them performing the many intricate tasks of balancing our internal systems and processes.

Likewise there are many, many different and effective responses to *the blues.* Diet and exercise are *major* factors, alongside reducing major external triggers, such as work stress. We all have things in our lives that we cannot change easily: our job, our relationship, our financial situation, the dependence that others in our lives have on us. We *can* change them, not by getting rid of them, but by changing the impact they have on us, and if we want to or need to then we can also slowly alter them entirely. There is no *single* response to depression, and to attempt to respond to it with recourse to only one treatment is simply foolish. Whilst prescription medicines are very effective in reducing symptoms, they represent only one of many things that can be done to mitigate a depressed mood; most of which are things you should do anyway just to maintain your happiness and keep yourself open to the possibilities the world has to offer.

So returning to the notion that ill-health stands in our way – well, yes and no. It can most certainly de-motivate and make many aspects of life very difficult; it can certainly by its very nature block the flow of purpose in our lives; but it can be dealt with in many circumstances, allowing us to open ourselves to that flow and to live a happy and fulfilling life once again.

Like many obstacles in our lives, illness is in large part only as big an obstacle as we perceive it to be. And as with the lack of money, there are always ways to walk in the direction of your goals that may be slower but are still moving you forward. If you are suffering some particular ill-health then I know you'll perhaps be struggling to accept this possibility, but equally likely, I hope, is that you've got this far through the book and maybe you are realising some things are worth giving a go regardless. Please try on what I'm saying for size, and even if it's a little tight or a little loose, maybe you'll make it fit better with a little time and wear.

You're afraid – Georgia O'Keeffe[8] said *I've been absolutely terrified every moment of my life and I've never let it keep me from doing a single thing that I wanted to do.* I could probably say the same.

I'm fortunate that courage is one of my main virtues; there's rarely much that holds me back from my goals. But that wasn't always the case. My childhood was very ordinary; *I* was very ordinary. I certainly wasn't endowed with barrels of confidence. I

[8] Georgia O'Keeffe was an American artist who lived to the age of 98; most well-known for her New Mexico landscapes and flowers.

think I always knew I was smart, although I didn't think other people thought so. I was socially awkward and certainly couldn't imagine any boys ever liking me. I didn't really know how to dress for any kind of effect, and my parents didn't have a lot of money to spend on clothes; there was never much money around at all. My mother even made many of my clothes.

I slowly started to prove my *smarts* to myself, and then developed more confidence by going into a sales career at a very young and green twenty-five. Ten years of sales heaped confidence, success and reputation on me. University study and parenthood added more. Executive management roles added more still, along with the ability to manage successful groups, make really cool stuff happen, converse with politicians and business leaders, motivate and inspire others, write well in all kinds of different mediums, and so on.

I made a bazillion mistakes and pissed off more people than I can count. I've feared for my career and my sanity, both more than once. I've been afraid of the next step and taken a deep breath and sucked it up many times over. I've not known what the next step is on many, many occasions.

What's the worst that can happen?

I'm also really good at thinking *What's the worst than can happen?* I'm not gung-ho and I am cautious, but so far, pretty much in none of my possible scenarios have I thought I might die. On the off-chance I might, I figure once I'm dead I'll no longer be worried. In all seriousness.

I've never been overly fussed about what others think about me; whilst it's hurt at times that others have judged me as they have, I can't think of a time that that's especially held me back. In fact it's frequently spurred me on.

Courage doesn't mean you're not afraid; it means you go ahead with your plans *despite* being afraid. Nine times out of ten, the scary thing doesn't turn out to be so scary at all, and it was just that you hadn't done it before that meant the unknown elements created a fear response. In the end, much of it is just a chemical reaction, a nervous response none of us have any control over.

I've twice hung upside-down over the turret of Blarney Castle in Ireland to kiss the blarney stone. If you don't know this, let me tell you: it's *really* high off the ground. There's someone holding onto you and there are bars that prevent you from falling the hundred or so feet to the ground *visible* below. Despite the virtual impossibility of falling, one's brain knows full well that one is hanging upside-down a hundred feet in the air and it reacts accordingly: it's terrifying. I did it anyway. **It was definitely a whole lot easier the second time around.**

Our fear also offers us hints for our own personal development, which in itself is a factor in living a life of purpose. It can be very interesting – and scary of course – to examine our fears. Indeed, one of our fears is to examine our fears. But go there, and see what you can see and learn. Mostly you will find your fears to be baseless, particularly once you've stepped on over to the other side of them.

Your Self-Talk is all negative – If you think poorly of yourself, if you put yourself down, if you think negatively about things generally, if you allow yourself to be down, if you just think about yourself *too much*, apart from giving yourself a challenge to be just plain happy, these views you have (about yourself in particular, but also about others) will literally stop your purpose coming to you. Putting those thoughts out there acts as a block to good things coming your way – it's literally like building a wall around yourself so that good things can't reach you. They cannot breach your own defences. You *must* think positively. This can be hugely difficult, I know. **We can be almost addicted to our negative thoughts** – the ones we have about ourselves as well as the ones we have about others. We can be so addicted that we'll tell ourselves we're just being realistic or honest about the way things are, or we'll believe we have a *right* to think what we want about others and even to express it. Let me stop you right there. If you believe you have a purpose, if you believe you're here to make a contribution, then it most certainly goes hand-in-hand with those two things that you are *not* here to be negative. From a purely spiritual point of view **you have no right whatsoever to be negative**, even about yourself. Please sit and soak this up for a while.

Making a concerted effort every day to *not* think negative thoughts and to instead think positive ones can be absolutely exhausting. That's just because you're not used to it. It's like any kind of exercise; if you start using muscles you've never used much they're going to complain. We all know what that kind of muscle ache feels like, when you can hardly sit down in a chair because your thighs scream at you, or you can't raise your arms above your head because your biceps scream at you. It's the same thing. Just like with screaming muscles, your negative thoughts will become easier to overcome. The first day you make a deliberate attempt *all* day to think positively and to *be* happy, you will probably feel it's going to just about kill you. The second day it gets a little easier – you maybe won't feel like you're going to die from it.

Practise being positive every day.

The thing is, with this thinking-positively business, again it's just like physical exercise in that you have to keep doing it. Every day. If you stop making a deliberate effort every day to be positive, then negativity will creep back in. If you get so good at being deliberately positive every day that you stop thinking about it so much, then the negative stuff will find its way back in there. Same as when you don't exercise every day. If you've been rigorous in exercising daily and you stop, then after a few days you'll already notice the difference. Don't stop. Never stop.

A word of warning… (There's always some fine print.) Don't over-do it. If you're totally over the top about being positive then you won't be being real.

You won't see the reality of things that do need addressing, like your relationship or your kids' behaviour or the way an employee is performing. Be positive, but be authentic. Be authentic, but be positive. I'm not overly keen on the exuberant practice of affirmations for this reason; it's not real. But then we Kiwis aren't given to that kind of exuberance either, so perhaps that's my culture expressing itself. Nonetheless, keep it real.

The things that stand in your way that you don't know about – There are some interesting and generally hidden challenges that most of us have that you're probably unaware act as quite significant obstacles in many areas of your life. Indeed these are often the *real* obstacles, and thus the real goals in living a life of purpose. They represent key personal development areas for most of us. You might be surprised by them; they are, in the main: judging, guilt, shame, holding onto the past, and not being able to forgive.

Judging – We *all* judge others; whether it's our co-workers, our relatives, our spouse, or the idiot that pulled out in front of us. We may judge our own children least of all, and ourselves harshest of all. We may have learned to keep our opinions of our co-workers and our relatives to ourselves, and we may exclaim loudly at the evening news, but whether it's unspoken or a frequent outrage, the judgement still exists.

We live in an era where social media expects us to have an opinion on every irrelevant soundbite that crosses our path, whether we're informed on all the facts surrounding it or not, whether we're even actually interested in it or not. Was the dress blue and black, or white and gold? Who cares?!

Separate yourself from erroneous, superficial and fickle judgement. Save your intuition and discernment for things that matter.

There is a specific area of discernment around this topic of judgement that it's important to grasp. Yes, you can judge that nuclear weapons are bad, and yes you can judge that the policies and practices of a particular government administration or regime are not to your liking, but the moment you make a mockery of someone, name and shame someone, refer to an entire group of people in a negative manner on the basis of one representative that you don't like, basically express your dislike in angry or bitter negative tones, then you're *judging* in the irrelevant and destructive way we're referring to judgement here. Wise up on the difference between expressing an opinion and doing so in a way that's insulting or offensive.

Guilt – Mothers seem to be the premier guilt group in society, but all of us seem to inherently and quite hold both individual guilt and/or some collective guilt for our particular demographic. Whatever guilt you hold and wherever it comes from, it does you precisely zero good at all, and in fact it causes you harm. Guilt is at the lowest level of spiritual experience, second only to shame. Guilt is a negative experience regardless of how you look at it. It bears no relationship to the act of taking responsibility for anything, despite the backward idea that the two must go hand in hand. *Guilty* in a legal sense doesn't mean you have to *carry* guilt; it means the law believes you did it, that's all. It's important to draw a distinction between *being* guilty in this sense, and *feeling* guilty. Feeling *remorse* is another thing too. We expect remorse from those who've done harm. The reality is that much of the individual guilt we carry has nothing to do with anything we did; possibly it's something we *think* we did, and that'll be because we've been expecting perfection from ourselves. You won't ever get it all right, especially as a parent, so just let that go and do the best you can without the guilt; guilt is not a thing you want to be passing onto your own children. Guilt is a waste of energy and it will stand in the way of happiness and purpose. And if you've suddenly just recognised that you've been passing guilt onto your children, don't suddenly load yourself up with more guilt because of that either. Seriously, you are doing yourself no good.

Shame – often goes together with guilt. Guilt is *I did something bad and I feel bad about it.* Shame is *I did something bad and I am the lowest excuse for a human being there is* or *Something bad was done to me and it's made me the lowest excuse for a human being there is.* Uh-uh! Shame is the lowest possible vibration; it has a negative value and will suck the goodness right out of everything. It is the single biggest block to happiness and purpose.

Like these other emotional obstacles, shame is a challenge to face and a challenge to move beyond, and will most likely require the support and guidance of a skilled coach. Confronting our shame necessarily involves opening the darkest box at the very back of our proverbial skeleton closet, which we may even have forgotten we put there (that being the idea, in all likelihood). We put it in that box way back there so we didn't ever have to look at it, and it's one of the hardest and bravest things we'll ever do to haul it out, open it up, take out the crap inside and deal with it. The light and space you create in your closet though is amazing. You will have room for the most wonderful new things that you'd never imagined you could look so good in before. You'll feel bold, confident, alive, attractive, likeable, and maybe even unstoppable. Wouldn't that be worth it?

Holding onto the Past – Many things hold our attention in our past rather than our present and future: the death of someone close, a bad work experience, abuse of many kinds, a relationship gone wrong, divorce, mistakes we've made or believe we've made; the list can be endless.

We *must* address the feelings we have for past events and move on, notwithstanding that that will still take time. Regardless of what holds us in the past, as long as it does then we are unable to be present here and now and consider our future clearly. We block the flow of love, positivity and purpose in the present simply because we're not *in* the present to receive them.

This is not the same as being able to enjoy happy memories from the past and share them; of course we will always have that relationship to the past. But we mostly go to that bit of our past happily and come back to the present easily. Events and people in our past that left us hurt or angry, that we can't let go of, tug at our hearts and souls and all but enslave them to reliving that hurt and anger over and over and over. **If you cannot let these things go, you will pay the price in lost opportunity and happiness in the present.**

But don't feel bad that you're stuck there – if you beat yourself up for not being able to let go then you're just piling more *stuff* on yourself. It will take time and once again probably the support and guidance of a counsellor, coach, or loving and wise friends. You'll get there. Be gentle on yourself.

Forgiveness – I've talked a lot about forgiveness in Chapter 2, as it is a key virtue to develop. The extent to which we don't forgive those we believe have harmed us (again, it really doesn't matter whether they really have harmed us or we just think they have – either way we can hold onto it and there's no value in that) is equal to the lessons we haven't learned from those encounters. So in other words, if there's some hurt you're hanging onto, then there's some lesson in there for you that you're going to understand better once you forgive; or alternatively once you understand it better then you can forgive it. *Not* forgiving – which implies that you're holding on to some hurt – is as much an obstacle to your spiritual development as any other negative feeling. Blocking your spiritual development will block your purpose.

Forgiveness is an art, and not one easily understood. If you have really enormous things from your past that you struggle to forgive, then I recommend my friend Di Riseborough's book *Forgiveness: How to Let Go When It Still Hurts*. Di describes the murder of her grandmother and the process she went through to forgive her grandmother's killer, including meeting him in prison. She offers very practical steps to negotiate forgiveness in this kind of massive life drama situation.

The biggest key to forgiveness, I think, is understanding what it means to forgive for *your* benefit, regardless of what it means for the person you choose to forgive. Forgiveness doesn't mean you excuse someone's behaviour – it does mean you're not going to let their behaviour continue to hurt you long after it occurred.

These latter four – guilt, shame, living in the past, and forgiveness – very often go together. We become stuck by events we blame ourselves for, or we cannot escape the hurt of things someone else has done. If you know one of these is affecting you, then do consider also where you sit with the other three, because they're almost certainly all sitting hidden in there altogether.

Finally, *lack of clarity* is an unexpected obstacle that can arrive when we think we've already got our purpose clear in our heads: out of the blue we can suddenly feel lost, confused, out of sorts, and we find ourselves questioning whether what we thought we were doing is the right thing after all. This is *really* common. Do not get upset about this. It can seem to happen *more* when you get clear, or as you're getting clearer. It's a strange phenomenon to explain, but the best I can put it is that it's some process of getting clearer still, whereby our mind and body is somehow expelling the 'unclearness' of our purpose; or that even greater clarity is emerging but it creates a whole lot of murkiness in the process. It's a little bit of *it has to get worse before it gets better*. The key to getting through these periods is to feel absolutely thrilled that you're clearing out some old lack-of-purpose dust, knowing everything's going to be really shiny and new and exciting once you're done with this bit of cleaning. My own experience, without exception, is that there is *always* some new revelation, some new refinement to my direction, after one of these kinds of periods. Mostly they just last a few days, but sometimes it's a few weeks, or even months; which can be hard to get through but I've learned to keep trusting the Universe just the same. Trust that you're still on your path and don't doubt yourself.

7 Obstacles are Lessons

Every single obstacle, real or imagined – and it doesn't make a lot of difference whether it's real or imagined since either way there's something needs sorting out – has a lesson in it. Sometimes the lesson is the problem itself and learning to overcome it – to learn the power of our mind and our spirit and our determination. Sometimes what we have to learn is more subtle.

If you don't have the money to do what you need to do – or you think you don't – either you have to realise that money isn't in fact the problem, or you have to get the money. Either way, you have something to figure out.

If you're afraid to leave home and travel overseas on your own, then you either have to figure what the very many reasons for being afraid might be – and there are many legitimate reasons to be cautious – or you have to just go anyway and overcome your fears along the way.

If you have been put off your goals by others' negative feedback, you either need to listen and learn from their feedback, figure out why you're letting their feedback hold you back, figure out how to not let it affect you, go ahead regardless, or all of the above.

If *you* are your own worst enemy, then you need to learn not to be, and instead learn to be your own best friend.

It can take a while before we even recognise the many criticisms we have of ourselves; sometimes they're very subtle. Amazingly, once we discover we have some and try to stop thinking and saying those things to ourselves, we'll then develop a new criticism of ourselves for not being able to stop telling ourselves negative things. And then when we realise we do that and we're *still* unable to stop the negativity all the time, then we'll criticise ourselves for that too.

Stop beating yourself up;
And stop beating yourself up
for beating yourself up;
And stop beating yourself up
for beating yourself up,
for beating yourself up!

Learning to overcome our own negative thinking is our biggest lesson in life. And most of us have it. Changing it will be something we're doing for the rest of our lives, albeit that it will get easier and more automatic the more we practise.

I'm of the opinion that in the process of ridding ourselves of the bulk of our negative thinking, we need to be gentle in the way we do it. Don't *hate* that part of yourself that feeds that negativity – not only does that kind of response have no value, but you're also not helping yourself by being negative to your negativity. We need to gently wave away the negative thoughts: *Oh it's you again – off you go – pfft!*

[Waves hand in air as though shooing a fly.] *Yes, it's nice to see you too, but I'd like my thoughts to be on* this *not* that, *thanks very much.* And then deliberately move your thoughts to something positive, kind, useful or constructive.

You will need to do this over and over and over. There may be days you feel you just can't summon the energy. Remember: all you have to do is move your mind from something negative to something positive, and keep doing it. Depending on how old you are and how many years you've been giving yourself these messages, it may be a good couple of years before you really notice that this change has become cemented, that the balance has shifted from negative to positive in your life. Learning this, and making it happen, is one of the most important lessons of your life. Along the way, you will make many other discoveries, as you cede the negative and grow the positive. Life will become lighter, happier, more relaxed, more successful, easier; in other words: *how it's meant to be.*

Don't deny yourself this ultra-important lesson – start now – be gentle with yourself. As you try and fail and try again, speak to yourself as you'd like the person you love to speak to you, as you might imagine an Angel might speak to you, with love and care and understanding, always there to say, *Let's try that again, shall we.*

What is the lesson in not having a clue what your purpose is? If you already believe you have one, then apart from the fact that that means you *are* now on your purpose journey, getting clear about it is a key part *of* it.

Here's the really simple answer: Since our purpose is a key aspect of our spiritual self, then it's the development of our spiritual self that will give us insight into our purpose. You will feed your spiritual self by expanding your spiritual education, by meditation and prayer, by being in nature and experiencing that particular kind of joy nature brings us, by relaxing deeply with many other practices such as yoga, mindfulness, and listening to Mozart; or even other activities and sports that can have a deeply relaxing effect: gardening, tinkering with engines if that's your thing, painting and sculpting. Primarily it is the activities of deep relaxation, prayer and meditation that power our spiritual self the most efficiently.

Just as when regular physical exercise energises us and provides us with more physical strength and get-up-and-go, regular spiritual exercise improves our spiritual get-up-and-go, and we begin to experience a more satisfying spiritual life, which will necessarily include more insight into our own life, a greater intuition, and more joy.

So if lack of clarity is your obstacle, then your lessons are a) to trust the process is still unfolding, and b) meditate and make sure you are doing everything possible to feed your spiritual Self.

If other commitments stand in your way, then you either need to clarify your priorities, or get organised, or find more time in the day, or know that the things you're doing right now *are* the things you're supposed to be doing right now and therefore are some part of your purpose, or all of the above. Sometimes it's hard to accept that some things we have to do are still a part of our purpose – almost certainly there is something to learn from it or it wouldn't be happening. Figure out what the lesson is, and you'll almost certainly find that time frees up for you sooner than you think.

I know many people who've been able to develop a new career or passion on less than an hour a day; if you want it, you can do it.

In the end though, living your purpose has little to do with time or money and everything to do with how you choose to live your life, with your personal development, and with your view of humanity and your contribution to it. Being able to live your purpose is not about finding your particular cause or some one special thing that will make all your dreams come true – this is as foolish as believing one person will make all your dreams come true.

***You* make your dreams come true, and your attitude towards what you are doing right now has more impact on your desire to be at purpose in your life than some future situation you imagine.**

You will do more for clarifying your sense of purpose by leaving the past and unburdening yourself of guilt and shame, than almost anything else.

It can sound trite and over-simplified to believe there is a lesson in everything that happens to us, I know. *What was the lesson for the small child that was sexually abused*, we may all well ask as one of the most obvious examples of what is otherwise a ridiculous belief that everything has a lesson in it. And the truth is I cannot answer that, for a number of reasons. I can't answer it because it's not within the scope of this book to answer it. I can't answer it because mere words can't explain it. I can't answer *you* if you ask the question, but I can answer myself, and I have, but please don't ask me to explain. What I can explain is there is not one single shitty thing that's happened to me in my life that I haven't been able to learn from and ultimately be grateful for. Not one. And some pretty shitty things have happened. I can't explain someone else's shit because it's not for me to understand – it's for them to. And so I offer you what I believe in, that there is a lesson in everything.

8 Your Purpose is Your Passion

This is probably one of the most obvious aspects of purpose. *Do what you love.*

Naturally we need to be sensible about it: watching YouTube videos and playing computer games all day is not generally one's purpose, although no doubt there are people who make careers out of testing new games for that enormous and growing part of the entertainment industry. Somehow or other you have to find something you love that also overlaps with that other key aspect: making a difference.

I've heard it suggested also that our purpose has to be the thing we're expert at, but actually that's not the case. My son has chosen a path to become a comedian. Whilst he has some natural talent, he's had to work hard at his craft and will probably have to continue working hard at it for many years before he becomes a professional comic. Likewise, my daughter wishes to be an artist; again she will probably have to work at it many years before it's able to sustain her. We all start off as amateurs.

You don't have to be an expert at the thing you love; you may even have only some small or intuitive sense of the thing you wish to achieve. Starting *somewhere* will increase the flow of positive energy around that choice, and inspiration, skill and opportunity will follow. Don't get too hung up on *where* to start – just start.

I've met many people who're stuck on knowing what their passion is, let alone their purpose. If you're not sure what your passion is, then you're going to need to spend time asking the Universe/the Divine for that particular inspiration. You can literally ask the question of God: *What is my purpose? Please show me my purpose.* This is where creating a daily connection to the Divine, to God, is vital. There are many ways to achieve that; meditation is without doubt the most effective.

If you've not learned to meditate, go to my FREE programme at http://suefitzmaurice.com/how-to-meditate-free-course. Not only will you learn how to meditate but you'll also get a lot of useful knowledge and information about the mechanics of meditating and how it can help you. Many people tell me they can't meditate because they can't stop thinking; they're usually surprised to hear that thinking's not in the least an obstacle to being able to meditate. In fact, thinking is very much *a part* of meditating.

One of the many ironies of purpose – and of life generally – is that you can also flip this entirely on its head and say that when you live with passion you will find your purpose. None of this is linear – I can't say to you: do this, then do this, then do this, etc, and you'll find your purpose. What I do know is that passion arises from purpose just as much as purpose arises from passion. If you live your life passionately, you open multiple doors to everything that promotes and inspires purpose. When you live passionately, you chase and grab hold of opportunities; you give your all to whatever you're doing no matter how mundane;

you go about every part of your work with good will
and humour; you're open to new experiences and
you're respectful and kind and engaging with
everyone you meet; you're interested in what's going
on in the world and you're interested in other people.
When you live your life this way – not complaining,
sincerely expressing your gratitude, loving whoever's
around to be loved – then your purpose will become
very clear to you.

Openness requires that you suspend judgment on
the possibilities of your life, and that even your
strongest beliefs can be up for grabs. If there is Truth
with a capital 'T' in the beliefs you hold dear, then
that Truth will stand the test of your openness to
change. Just as you cannot have a purposeful life
without passion, you cannot have a passionate life
without openness.

If there is really *nothing* you have a passion for,
then your task is not to find your purpose despite this,
but in fact to develop passion. Do something new, go
somewhere new, talk to someone new. Do something
you do every day in a different way. Surprise someone
you see every day. Take a different route to work, try
a new recipe the like of which you've never tried
before. *Learn to meditate.* Move the furniture around;
move house! Definitely try and do things that are
outside your comfort zone – there is nothing as useful
to our personal development as challenging ourselves
to do something that scares us.

We must *live* in order to have passion and purpose.
If some passion for living is not present in your life,

then happiness and fulfilment are unlikely to appear either.

If you have multiple passions and you're confused about which direction to take, then my advice is don't try to decide directly yourself. There is a gift in allowing the path to take you where it will, and see where you end up. And there is no need to obsess on the idea that just one thing has to be *the* thing. The more you tune into your spiritual self, the clearer things will become for you. Like most good things in life, gaining clarity takes the time it takes, and you will do well to allow it time. I have felt a sense of urgency about my life, for most of its first fifty years, and whilst passion, commitment, hard work and courage have stood me in good stead, impatience rarely has. Impatience is not a comfortable feeling and it necessarily carries with it an insufficient gratitude for, and pleasure in, what one has now. I have little of this impatience left lately; it steadily disappeared the more I practiced gratitude for what was going on in my life in the here and now. It's a relief to be rid of it. When we're younger, of course, we naturally seem to have more impatience – we want to get on with our lives and see the world and gain our independence. Part of this arises as a natural part of youth, but part of it arises from pressure to achieve certain things also. As with teaching our youth how to find their purpose, we neglect also to teach them the great value of allowing life to unfold and trusting it do so, just as the days and seasons pass and roll into the next one. We're too much in a hurry, and the reality of living like that is that we chase our tails and go nowhere fast. Puppies and kittens are supposed to chase their tails –

we're not. They enjoy it (and we enjoy watching them), but most of us find no pleasure in that frenzied feeling.

If you know what you love, and you know it's your purpose, but you don't seem to be able to make it happen in your life, go through the *Obstacles* section again. Be patient and believe.

If your impatience arises from wanting your new business idea to happen, it's not a part of this book to talk about marketing yourself, your business idea, your brilliant invention, and so on, but if that's where you're at and it's not working, please get good advice and professional business help. Aside from that, you still have to allow the Universe time. Give time the time.

Sometimes we find our passion slipping for the thing we've loved doing for years. Many of us have experienced this in the middle or latter parts of our working lives in particular, and possibly you're just coming back around to the beginning of a new purpose. It can be a bit of a shock and a key contributor to the proverbial mid-life crisis, and can include a sudden loss of personal meaning and fulfilment. There's no denying how unsettling this can be; it's broken up many marriages, destroyed people's financial independence, and left folk depressed and even suicidal. We crave meaning and usefulness; for many women this change occurs as their children grow up and leave home. For others, the goal posts just shift and we find we need a different type of fulfilment. Very long gone are the days when we stayed in the same job or career until retirement. When we find ourselves in this position, we come back again to the first proposition of this book which is pretty much *What is the meaning of life?* And the answer remains *To find your purpose and live it.*

9 You *Are* Living a Life of Purpose

Just by picking up this book, by having the intention to live a life of purpose, you are already living a life of purpose. When it is your intention every day to live purposefully, then you've already embarked on that journey by being in the here-and-now and by simply having that intention. Intention has a powerful energy. When you desire something strongly you are inviting the Universe to respond to you. It will almost certainly not respond in the manner you'd intended, but it will respond. And it will keep responding as long as that intention remains.

Living a life of purpose has a great deal to do with desire, and by our ability to go beyond ourselves for what we seek: to look to the Divine, to look at how we may serve others, to look at what contribution we can make. Everything positive we project helps to create purpose. Everything negative blocks purpose and blocks happiness.

You will not manage to stay positive all the time; the very process of letting go of shame, guilt, and judgment necessarily throws us into those feelings; just as the very process of purposeful living will from time to time throw us into confusion. It is some inherent part of healing that things sometimes get worse first, and so it is with purpose and happiness. As our hearts and souls release attachment to the past, attachment to judgment, all of these things, then we will at times find ourselves in the depths of experiencing them, and this can make for some challenging times in moving into happiness and into purpose. I have found, perhaps oddly, that if I don't fight these experiences or beat myself up because this feels like a backward step, and even more if I do my best to express my gratitude for this evolving moment, then those moments of fear and pain move on much more quickly and there is almost always something wonderful on the other side.

Living a life of purpose has to do with being on the path of purpose, not having got to the end of the walk. We rarely, if ever, know in a flash what our purpose is and then set out living it and that's the whole story. Living our purpose has to do with finding it, allowing it to unfold, removing the obstacles to it, reinforcing its development and clarity with various daily practices, and tuning into its shifts and enhancements, throughout our lives. If your intention is to live a life of purpose, then you are.

Finale

We all do all of the things that block our purpose from time to time. Nobody's perfect. It's not about keeping score, and it's not that we're expected to be wary of everything we do in every second. But the extent to which we can limit the expression of that which limits us, and expand the expression of that which expands us, will affect the clarity of our purpose and our ability to live it.

Living your purpose is fundamentally about developing yourself and your personal traits and virtues, and making a contribution. It is a spiritual pursuit in the manner of Maslow's self-actualization, in that our purpose goes beyond just our intellectual, emotional and social fulfilment; it's a thing that goes to the very core of who and what we are.

Entrepreneur Aaron Hurst says we are now living in a *purpose economy*,[9] where our work criteria of personal development and being able to contribute our time and talent to meaningful work that makes a difference, now dominate the work sphere. No particular demographic has a monopoly on it either. It is not the pursuit solely of the rich, the white, the Christian, the Westerner, the educated, or any particular gender.

It's almost as though Maslow's hierarchy could be applied to the whole of humanity and we are now in the *era* of self-actualization, the era of being able to

---

[9] Hurst, Aaron (2014) *The Purpose Economy*. Boise, Idaho. Elevate.

rise above ourselves and look at what difference we can make for our planet. We are on the path to self-actualization as a species. And not before time.

Acknowledgements

I am deeply grateful to the love and support of an extraordinary bunch of women collectively gathered on Facebook as the Inspirational Page Owners Group. We have been together for more than three years during which time all manner of collective projects have arisen among members. They have been my saviours and my sanity on many an occasion. Thank you especially to Kathryn Yarborough, Fiona Childs, Lynda Field, Caryn Dudarevitch, Allison Sara, Heather McCloskey Beck, Jenn Manning, Eleanor Brownn, Nancy Rainwater, Chanal Brunner, Michelle Inman Quesada, Linda Pollock and Laurel Bleadon-Maffei.

My extra special thanks to Swati Nigam for her beautiful guidance, wisdom, and great generosity of spirit.

Sarah McCrum has been my closest mentor over the last decade and challenged me more than anyone. I could not have got to here without you, Sarah.

I am blessed to have some exquisite people in my life, most especially Sue 2, Ra and Paora. Thank you for your love and friendship, for accompanying me on my journey lately and for allowing me to accompany you on yours.

My two children remain my greatest inspiration and blessing, and as they enter adulthood two of my most important teachers. No one calls me out on my behaviour more than my children, and whilst they have been known to wound me more than anyone ever could on occasion, they are secretly my greatest fans and my biggest supporters, and I say that knowing they love me for more than just my grocery shopping, taxi cab and laundry skills.

About the Author

Sue was born and raised in New Zealand. She has been a nurse, a CEO, an executive business consultant and coach, and is the mother of a teenage son and daughter pursuing careers as a comedian and an artist respectively. Sue has degrees in philosophy and political science, and international law and international relations; and a Masters in Business. She is currently a PhD candidate.

She is the author of *Angels in the Architecture,* a novel, inspired by her severely autistic nephew. The book began with the idea that there is more going on in the heads of autists than we generally think, and it grew into an historic tale, a discussion on prejudice and an exploration of our beliefs about what is real and what we can truly know.

Sue coaches and lectures on healing depression, and living purposefully.

Follow Sue:
www.SueFitzmaurice.com
www.facebook.com/SueFitzmauriceAuthor

Made in the USA
Lexington, KY
09 October 2015